TALENT
PROPHECY

RUSSELL KLOSK

TALENT PROPHECY

Creating Strategic Impact

Through **Workforce Planning**

and **Talent Strategy**

Forbes | Books

Published by Forbes Books, Charleston, South Carolina.
An imprint of Advantage Media Group.

Forbes Books is a registered trademark, and the Forbes Books colophon is a trademark of Forbes Media, LLC.

Printed in the United States of America.

10 9 8 7 6 5 4 3 2 1

ISBN: 979-8-88750-425-4 (Hardcover)
ISBN: 979-8-88750-426-1 (eBook)

Library of Congress Control Number: 2024904889

Cover design by Matthew Morse.
Layout design by Ruthie Wood.

This custom publication is intended to provide accurate information and the opinions of the author in regard to the subject matter covered. It is sold with the understanding that the publisher, Forbes Books, is not engaged in rendering legal, financial, or professional services of any kind. If legal advice or other expert assistance is required, the reader is advised to seek the services of a competent professional.

Since 1917, Forbes has remained steadfast in its mission to serve as the defining voice of entrepreneurial capitalism. Forbes Books, launched in 2016 through a partnership with Advantage Media, furthers that aim by helping business and thought leaders bring their stories, passion, and knowledge to the forefront in custom books. Opinions expressed by Forbes Books authors are their own. To be considered for publication, please visit **books.Forbes.com**.

This book is for my soulmate Carolyn Ford, loving wife and mother, and my fiercest supporter taken far too soon.

To my daughters Vivian and Lydia to show pouring your soul into what you believe in lets you achieve it. To the family, friends, coworkers, and others who have loved and supported me in good times and bad and helped me to be more than I ever thought possible.

CONTENTS

INTRODUCTION

Hewlett-Packard, or HP for short, was founded in 1939 by Bill Hewlett and David Packard; the company would eventually become one of the juggernauts of the personal computing era. In fact, from 2007 to 2013, HP was the biggest PC manufacturer in the world. In 2009, the company ranked ninth on the Fortune 500 list.

Around that time, the company had almost 350,000 employees, served customers in more than a hundred countries, and brought in around $120 billion in revenue each year. But there was trouble on the horizon. Between 1947 and 1999, HP had only four CEOs. Over the next fifteen years, they went through six.

Part of the problem was HP's desire to transition from its traditional focus on its products into services. As the personal computer and printer that had made HP a dominant player became commoditized—after all, there was little difference between an HP computer and a Dell or Lenovo—HP thought they could maintain that dominance by pivoting to cloud services and system integration delivery.

This was a reasonable strategy, but HP made a critical mistake. They decided to focus their service strategy on affordability over quality. In other words, they wanted to be a low-cost competitor instead of a high-quality one. This was the era when tech was first becoming infatuated with offshoring talent, and HP figured they could staff their service division primarily outside the United States, save on labor costs, and undercut their competition.

It didn't work out that way.

HP had a plan of sorts. They already had some presence in places like India, Costa Rica, Argentina, and other offshore hubs with large amounts of tech talent. They intended to expand their footprint in these places where they knew they could hire the necessary talent. With that plan in mind, they sold IT services contracts to companies at a rate that would be profitable—if their workforce planning was in order. Delivered from offshore, these contracts would profit HP and save money for the customers.

We can see how this planning let them down by considering their contract. This was a standard servicing with a large financial services institution based in the southern United States. The contract covered not just physical technology but apps and other digital solutions. In theory, the only HP presence that had to be located in America was direct tech support.

The problem HP ran into was that the company didn't yet have enough staff hired in Costa Rica—or the facility to house them. While HP built up their presence there, they had to run services through their offices in the United States. For two years, HP supported the contract out of places like Charlotte, Atlanta, and New York. By the time HP was ready to transition to their new Costa Rican office, the bank was not interested in making the change. After all, they were getting great service at an incredible price without any of the controversy of using offshore workers.

Such poor judgment on workplace planning and talent strategy spread across the company. This added extra pressure at the top of the organization, where HP was carrying a significant debt load while the market was slowing down. The company started burning through

CEOs, with each new leader making very dramatic efforts to turn things around. With all this desperate fumbling, the company began missing Wall Street earning targets. And then the financial crisis further slowed business. Leadership began to panic.

What followed was a series of layoffs. Eventually, after multiple rounds of cuts, the company went from 350,000 employees to a low of 287,000. With such dramatic layoffs, it was impossible to hold on to top talent, and that left the company without the resources to arrest the downward spiral. In 2015, the company split into two, creating HP, Inc. for its products and Hewlett Packard Enterprises for its services. And thus ended HP's efforts to pivot to services—undone by poor workforce planning.

The Risk of Poor Planning

It didn't have to go that way. I was part of the team working within HP at the time to build a workforce planning model that would have allowed the company to shift its talent resources to accommodate the new focus on services. It was true they needed some cuts—by my estimate they had about 32,000 more employees in certain areas than they needed. But they also needed to hire people with the skills of tomorrow, maybe as many as 18,000 new people for other positions. For instance, to make that strategy work, for every two computer programmers they cut in Charlotte, they needed to hire a DevOps person in Costa Rica.

If they'd followed this strategy on a reasonable timeline, the company could have remained successful. Unfortunately, HP didn't follow the model. And they paid for it.

This is not to say they didn't have very talented leaders—they did. It is to say that the differentiator in an information age is talent and talent strategy. Talent decisions are what drive success and failure far more so than global supply chains or union versus non-union factories. And if leadership can't come to terms with that dynamic, it can put even very large and successful companies at risk.

If this could happen to HP, it could happen to any company. No matter how strong your brand or how impressive your revenue or how outstanding your products or services, you have to take the risks associated with poor workforce planning and talent strategy very seriously.

I've been in this industry for decades, and I've seen the same story play out time and time again across industries. Fellow tech giant IBM made similar mistakes in the early 2000s. Leadership misunderstood the state of offshoring their highly skilled workforce. They moved many of their operations to India, assuming the lower labor costs would drive down overall costs, lower prices on their products, and improve their profit margins. What they didn't consider was that such a move put them in direct competition with companies that had very different labor costs.

The labor cost models of the Indian outsource providers are estimated by *Intelligent Sourcing* and other industry publications to be about a third of the cost of providers in Europe or the United States. This is true not just of client-facing labor but executive and back-office costs as well.

However, if you set up delivery centers in India, you can match some of the labor costs, but you will still have your overhead functions at a higher cost. Additionally, if a US-based firm wishes to compete in this space, the differentiation to the client cannot just be financial. Service and innovation have to be the differentiation, and that requires different skills and different levels of experience in your workforce than what the offshore competitors can offer.

IBM ran into similar problems in its efforts. The company eventually recovered but only after years of pain.

Here's another example: a large, successful tech consulting company I've worked with has a fifty-year corporate history. Over that entire history, the company has only missed Wall Street estimates five times. Three of those five have been in the last three quarters. Another may be coming as they forecast slower growth.

These issues aren't driven by the economy or the quality of their product. The root cause can be found in decisions leadership made about their workforce. They made the mistake of overpaying for talent at the bottom of their ladder while laying off talent at the top. This had a short-term benefit of impressing Wall Street with reduced payroll after cutting those big salaries. But the longer-term consequences were written on the wall. Sales and product differentiation suffered, as well as the reputation of the firm.

Once again, leadership justified this decision by building IT systems abroad. Unfortunately, they began building this infrastructure and hiring this workforce as cloud was scaling and AI capabilities came to market. Suddenly, their competitors were reshoring this work, and their clients were bringing much of it back in-house—in both cases because the work required a smaller workforce and could be handled affordably onshore.

While their competitors were hiring more high-end talent with more hands-on industry expertise—the sort this company had just let go—they discovered they'd sunk massive costs into the wrong labor strategy. As with IBM, this company will be fine, but they're in for some pain in the near term.

To be clear, this book is agnostic on offshoring as a business strategy. There are times when it is useful and even necessary. There are other times when it's the wrong call. I am also not claiming that workforce planning was the only cause of the turbulence these companies faced. The point of the stories I've shared here is that *any* major business strategy is less likely to succeed if you don't first understand the talent you have, the talent you need, and the strategies to make the two meet.

And this is true across the whole economy. While all three of these companies are in the tech sector, the risks and rewards of workforce planning and strategy are the same across every industry. The issues HP and IBM faced are the same issues you'll find at McDonald's or Walmart or JPMorgan Chase. The specific labor requirements and specific business strategies are different, but the principles remain the same.

Prediction and Data

In business, when things are going well, it's easy to feel invulnerable at times. You shoot past expectations quarter after quarter, and you dominate your industry. Attracting talent appears effortless. It feels like nothing could take you down. But fortune can turn around very quickly, and if you don't have excellent workplace planning and talent management strategies in place, you expose yourself to the risks that brought down HP.

Before going any further, let me take a moment to define these concepts here. According to the International Organization of Standardization, workforce planning is:

A process that ensures people with the appropriate skills are in the right place, at the right location, at the right time to meet the customers' changing needs. It examines what an organization needs to accomplish in a given period of time; what knowledge, skills, and experience are required to get the job done; and how large a workforce and what type of workforce are required to provide that mix of skills, knowledge, and experience.

Talent management, meanwhile, is defined as "the process of developing and integrating new workers, developing and retaining current workers, and attracting highly skilled workers to an organization."

Luckily, it is now possible to model both components to match your labor needs while also developing powerful, accurate predictability in how those needs will shift over time. You can anticipate ahead of time the results of adjustments of your workforce planning and talent. Imagine if you could know whether reducing employee turnover would have a positive or negative affect on everything from the bottom line to employee morale, customer satisfaction, innovation, and product development. Knowing the outcome before you disrupt the organization or spend the money is a question of modeling—a question not dramatically different from how an actuary works to price a life insurance policy.

The essence of talent acquisition and management has always been about the right people, the right place, with the right skills at the right time and right price. Now, you can help ensure you get these decisions right with data that offers predictable and forecastable results for your organization. Such results can have a high degree of efficacy necessary for data-driven business decisions.

In fact, with the *right* data and the *right* modeling, you can now know where the problems are at the job level and give yourself near certitude in your actions. Of course, we can't predict everything. We'll never be able to know if George in sale acquisition will leave his position this year or if Sarah in customer support will fit well when shifted into a new role in HR, but we can know with about 80 percent certitude that of all the Georges and Sarahs in your organization, around thirty will leave and all but around fifteen will adjust to their departments. What's more, we can know that you'll need another five Georges and three Sarahs over the next year—and potentially how many you have to bring in each quarter.

Essentially, you can put rigor and evidence-based data behind HR functions. With visibility in your data and structure in your workforce planning, you can remove much of the gut-instinct decision-making that's so prevalent even in most successful corporations.

It's hard to overemphasize how big a deal this is. Since the beginning of corporate business, there's been difficulty finding any certainty over hiring and retention needs. It's a constant struggle to move talent around organizations. There are chronic issues with over-staffing in one department and understaffing in another.

Now, it's possible to have true visibility in your workforce—across a single department or scaled all the way to the enterprise level. The technology already available enables this visibility at a cost previously thought not possible. These days, this is not a technology problem; it is a process and governance one. And those processes and governance models can be built and deployed surprisingly quickly once you understand the concepts behind them.

Workforce predictability has many knock-on benefits, including happier employees, higher retention, improved production, and, ultimately, more revenue. Making sure your people have what they need when they need it is both more rewarding for them and allows you to execute your business strategy—whatever that strategy is.

It can also allow you to hire with more precision across time and location. Imagine the benefits of being able to tell your HR department not "We need a thousand new people this year" but "We need two hundred new people in quarter one across these three divisions and these two locations, another three hundred in quarter two across these four divisions, and in these specific jobs, etc." Imagine the confidence with which you'll make future decisions when those predictions prove right.

Workforce Needs Change Over Time

When the robots came for those jobs in the 1980s, some people assumed this was the end of the car manufacturing job. It seemed in the moment that technology would eventually eliminate the factory workforce entirely, opening the gates for massive profits, lower costs, and a future without any need for the concerns of this book.

We all know that reality never came to pass. Instead, while the plant requires fewer employees now, those workers all earn far higher salaries. A car plant may now have three hundred employees instead of three thousand, but the savings on workforce aren't particularly significant, as the workers of today have higher labor costs relative to the economy than the workers of the 1970s. Instead, those jobs that were once labor focused now require knowledge workers who can demand higher pay for their skills.

This is the nature of workforce dynamics. Disruption occurs in technology, customer behavior, or economic realities, and businesses have to adjust their hiring, retention, and resource policies quickly if they want to stay ahead. This was the source of HP's trouble. The company correctly saw the future was in services, but it couldn't adjust its workforce to meet that shift.

This is also your dilemma. We don't yet know where the next disruption will come from. It may be in advances in AI. It could be a definitive shift away from the Chinese market. It could be the emergence of the African continent as a major source of labor or growing markets. It could be changes in emissions standards. It could be something we haven't yet even thought of.

But it will be your job to make sure your workforce can adjust to that new reality. The only trend we can be confident will remain in place is the focus on skills and knowledge over labor. Whatever shift occurs, you will want the best people with the most experience, talent, and knowledge in the ideal positions within your company. You'll want them working with people who can allow them to produce the best results.

You'll need your company to be agile in attracting those people, placing them, shifting them around the organization, and replacing them if they leave. And that means that workforce planning and talent strategies have to be at the forefront of your thinking.

Modeling Workforce Made Easy

The ideas in this book are necessary if you want to ride the waves of disruption ahead, but that doesn't mean the path forward is easy. I won't lie to you, the math behind the models in this book is intimidating. You will need talented data scientists on hand to tackle it.

But I suspect you already have data scientists. What you lack is the high-level understanding to lead the implementation of these ideas into your business. That's what we're going to do here.

This book is not academic or technical in terms of the mathematics behind it. Instead, my aim is to offer an approachable, actionable process that will allow you to assess workforce needs, develop a workforce plan, and engage in strategic talent management.

To effectively plan, you will need significant data, but here, disruptive technology offers us a new way forward. For instance, we've known since the beginning of time how to assess skills. Historically, it's done in one of two ways. Either I ask you what your skills are, and you rate yourself on them, or I ask your manager what your skills are, and they rate you. There are obvious flaws in either system. In particular, they're time-consuming, open to bias, and people can game the system. These options also don't account for skills outside the remit of the current position—and those may be the skills you're most in need of.

But now, we have new technological tools. We have LinkedIn and other social media sites where people post about the skills they have and the degrees that they possess. We have AI, which can scrape those sites to collect that data. We have the cloud where we can store far more data for analysis.

Again there's a lot of math behind this analysis, but you don't need to understand it in order to have your teams implement it—you just need to understand the ideas themselves. That's where we're going to go in this book. We'll discuss the science behind predictable workforce planning, the table-stakes ideas you have to accept for these ideas to bear fruit, and the system itself that will allow you to use your data to make workforce decisions with far greater confidence.

By the end, you'll know all that these ideas can do for you and exactly what you need your team to deliver in order to install these strategies in your business.

Unleash Incredible Potential

As a vice president of HR at Hewlett-Packard I saw the company fall apart in real time. I also saw IBM make its workforce mistakes. But in my long career, I've seen more successes than failures. In my thirty-two years working with and consulting for Fortune 500 companies, I've seen great results at Microsoft and PricewaterhouseCoopers. I've been in the trenches with companies across six continents and in industries as diverse as tech, financial services, products, retail, and travel—seeing the very best and worst workforce planning on the planet.

All that experience has taught me two things. First, you cannot afford to ignore workforce planning or talent strategy. And second, if you implement a well-designed system, you can unleash truly incredible results that will differentiate you from your competitors both to your employees and to your customers through products you put in the marketplace.

How incredible? Let me tell you.

You may have heard of a little startup called Moderna. Along with Pfizer, they led the way to synthesizing the COVID vaccine using new mRNA technology. What you may not know is that one of the reasons they were so well placed to keep up with massive companies like Pfizer and Johnson & Johnson is because of their elite workforce planning.

About a decade ago Moderna was simply a new company with a different mindset looking to shake the industry up. But their talent management didn't reflect that mindset. Back then, they were still running a very traditional five-hundred-person company. It was impossible for them to keep up with the research spending of the Johnson & Johnsons of this world following the same playbook. They simply didn't have the resources for that.

But if they implemented elite workforce planning and talent strategy, they were far more likely to get where they wanted to go—and they were likely to get there about three years quicker.

"You're an R&D company, so what would those three years get you? In pharmaceuticals, they get you everything."

I told something similar to Moderna's competitor Merck in one meeting. This is one of the heavyweights of the industry that Moderna was trying to displace. In any given year, they might spend $2 billion on research and development. But R&D is expensive. For Merck, at that time, that might allow them to get ten to twelve potential drugs through clinical trials. What could workplace planning do? It might up that total to twelve to fourteen drugs without raising the costs at all—simply by optimizing how resources were leveraged and deployed and how skills could be more tightly aligned to different phases of the clinical development.

Another prominent chemical company that I've worked with—which would prefer to remain unnamed—may have recently unlocked a cure for blindness. Their solution uses the same materials in their artificial heart valves to make the eye membrane that protects an Intel microchip that connects to the optical nerve.

That revolutionary idea was developed by four brilliant scientists. But the company would never have made this breakthrough if they didn't have the right four scientists in the right room at the right time with the right resources.

This is the kind of potential that workforce planning can unleash. Poorly done, it can doom one of the biggest corporations on the planet. Done well, with the right tools and the right models, it can change the world. Whatever industry you're in, if you can get the right people in the right place at the right time, right cost, and right skills, you can unlock incredible breakthroughs.

To secure that kind of potential for your organization, the first step is reading on.

PART I

THE SCOPE OF THE PROBLEM

CHAPTER 1

The Science of Predicting Workforce Needs

Cencora, previously known as AmerisourceBergen, controls a large percent of the middle market for pharmaceuticals in America. It is essentially a warehouse company that stores the drugs produced by pharmaceutical companies and prepares them for shipments to doctors and hospitals. Cencora and its competitor, McKesson, are the dominant players that make sure drugs get where they need to be when they need to be there.

Think of Cencora as a specialized Amazon. It's more complicated because there are strict laws and oversight governing drugs and their distribution, as well as complex climate requirements for some drugs. But in all other respects, the company's warehouses are run like any other warehouse. There are standard shifts in which employees take orders, fill them, and prepare them for shipping to various locations.

On a surface level, it seems like this should be very simple to schedule. Cencora could run two shifts, the first from 8 a.m. to 5 p.m. and the second from 3 p.m. to 11 p.m. The first shift would come in, take care of overnight orders, handle incoming orders and—theoretically—leave the afternoon orders for the second shift. The second shift paid 10 percent more because it was less convenient for most people.

The company had a mandatory overtime policy designed for emergencies and because of the criticality of getting drugs out to hospitals and pharmacies overnight. As you can imagine, a lot of the demand for drugs comes in later in the day as nonelective surgeries are scheduled and prescriptions processed by drugstores in the normal course of a business and patient care. Over time, though, that policy began being used excessively, as labor demand was far outstripping supply and the realities of supply chain and logistics management meant that Sunday, Monday, and Tuesday became surge days in the afternoon. Exacerbated by a tightening job market, the mandatory overtime policy became foundational to the business model just to keep standard shipments running smoothly. And the majority of the extra hours were falling on one particular shift. While second-shift workers kept close-to-normal hours, first-shift workers were working sixty to seventy hours every week. Overtime can be a great bonus occasionally with the time-and-a-half that comes with it, but when it becomes standardized it leads to burnout, and this leads to huge amounts of churn—as well as excess cost to the business.

The company tried various ways to resolve this churn on their own. In particular, they'd raised their hourly wage. Up to a certain point, this did net them some more people, but they found there were diminishing returns above that point. The reason was simple: Those people who expect to make a significant hourly wage also want better working conditions than a warehouse.

Cencora had also expanded their temporary workforce to include local college students and others who would take shifts here and there as they wanted or needed them. But that created extra chaos in the system since they couldn't count on consistent labor to cover the shifts.

Enter the consultants. After reviewing their data, two issues became apparent. The first was an easy fix. Cencora weren't organizing their orders by volume. Some drugs were shipped in huge quantities, but they weren't given priority placement in the warehouses. They might be in spot 24B when spot 2A held drugs in much lower demand. Reorganizing based on volume could net them some time saved over a week. That fix was well within their capabilities and the existing capabilities of their inventory management system, so it was quickly moved upon.

But that wasn't the main issue. The main issue was a misalignment between schedules and when the orders came in. The data on this was very clear. On an average morning, the first half of the first shift was steady, smooth, untaxing. Primarily, time was spent receiving shipments from the manufacturers for storage until needed. The team focused on fulfilling orders that had come in overnight, but those were far fewer than what would come in during the day. Most of the orders for the day started not at 8 a.m. or 10 a.m. but around noon. This makes sense when you stop to think about it. Other than elective surgeries, most orders are going to start coming in as patients are seen, starting in the morning.

This led to a situation in which the warehouse was a slow-paced work environment until orders started really building up—usually around 3 p.m. From then on, it was chaotic until 9 p.m. when the logistics companies (UPS, FedEx, etc.) would arrive to haul away the packed trailers. Those who started at 8 a.m. had a relatively easy job until 3 p.m., but then they had to stay on through the rush every shift.

Once this was clear, the solution became fairly obvious. Align the shifts to when the demand was needed and intentionally overlap. Cencora sought to split up the first shift so that a third of it still came in at 8 a.m. The rest worked from 1 p.m. to 9 p.m. The second shift still worked 3 p.m. to 11 p.m. Cencora paid a small differential to those who moved to the new middle shifts and offered some help accommodating the life change—such as working with parents to find daycare options. But it was all worth it. The overtime shrank to a manageable level almost overnight, turnover was reduced, and the constant churn disappeared.

The Math Behind Workforce Planning

This may seem a fairly simple example of workforce planning and management, but that is my point. When you have the right data and right models in place, solutions become far easier to see and game out. This same clarity is possible when your data is run through the system shared in this book. It doesn't matter if you're working with blue-collar labor or white-collar knowledge workers. It doesn't matter if you're dealing with shifts or attempting to place the right experts in the right team. You can predict need and find solutions as straightforwardly as Cencora—and you can have confidence you've got the formula right.

While the characteristics of the workers have changed over time, every business has faced the age-old problem of finding the right people in the right place with the right skills at the right cost and at the right time. In the past, companies had to make massive corrections because they had no way to compute the trends at play. They'd over-hire on talent, end up with a glut, and have to do layoffs. Or they'd struggle with a massive talent shortage and desperately try to fill it at any cost.

That's no longer the case. The plain truth today is that well-run companies rarely do layoffs. The market can certainly create staffing shortages, but they can be predicted, with the mediations modeled out so that viable solutions are achieved. In fact we can forecast—in some cases years in advance—what those shortages will be, model how we will avoid them, and then execute talent strategy to mitigate that risk long before problems arise. These days, we can back up recruitment, organization, and promotion decisions with science. We can model what happens next with the workforce you have and what your workforce needs to look like in the future. We can discover what issues likely lie ahead and how you should respond to them. We can model how to hit your targets at the right cost while remaining competitive.

While there are limits to predictability—humans being what they are, you'll never be 100 percent certain any one person will do anything—with the right models in place, you can make decisions with about 80 percent certainty. This is achievable because modeling is done at a job level, through a lens of relevant skills, and is independent of any specific individual. You can model what you will need, when, and where, as well as optimize the cost to obtain or develop talent. Taken forward, this informs not only what work is done but where it is done and by what type of worker.

The math behind these models is intimidating to a non-mathematician, but it's perfectly within the capabilities of the data scientists you already have working for you. To access the fruits of this science, all you need now is a simplified understanding of the mechanics behind these models. And that can be presented in a way anyone can understand. In fact, with the right models and the right tools, this information can affordably and easily be put in the hands of line managers and utilized in the micro- and macro-environment to optimize how work is performed.

I know that because that's how it was initially explained to me. When I was first learning about the math and science behind workforce planning, my head was swimming. I've always been very good at math, but this felt beyond. That's when someone took me aside and said they could teach it to me over a forty-five-minute lunch.

I was in a conference room in San Francisco at the time, where I was being taught stochastic math (or multivariable optimization). This was, in essence, third-semester college calculus. Yes, I had an aptitude for it and had passed multiple calculus classes in college, but in that class, I was taught the same way a high school student would be, and it was easy to understand the concepts.

And that means, even if you don't share my aptitude for math, you can understand the concepts behind these models. With your team of data scientists and this basic understanding, models can then be calculated in computer software and under the old adage "Garbage in = garbage out." Understanding these concepts will allow you to make sure the right information is put into the machine. That enables you to trust the output and execute your talent management processes against those outputs. Things a line manager, regardless of profession, can do if the models are built correctly.

As everyone else left to get something to eat, he laid it out this way:

Imagine you run a supermarket. As the manager, you set a priority to never have more than three people waiting in line at a time. Now, let's say you have fifteen cash registers available. Two cashiers are on registers at all times. If volume increases, and you end up with four or more people waiting in each line, your front-end manager comes out and asks another employee to open a third register.

We all see this in stores every day. And over time, you can learn to predict volume in the store and schedule to make sure you have enough cashiers available to step in before the lines lengthen. You'll know that Saturday and Sunday afternoons are always busy with shoppers, so you need to schedule more cashiers for those hours. On the other hand, Monday morning is going to be very slow, and it'd be a waste of money to have more than two or three cashiers working those hours.

We're back in Cencora territory here, and it feels very simple because this is basic linear algebra. It's A + B = C kind of stuff. And this is often how supermarkets actually work out their labor needs and scheduling.

However, if we want to more fully model reality, we have to move beyond the linear algebra we all understand. The reason for this is that in a real supermarket, as in any real business, there are more variables than just time and cost. To model those extra variables, we have to use something called stochastic math, which is third-semester calculus.

In your supermarket, you don't just have the number of cashiers and the cost of paying them to consider. You also have the staff in other departments. You have the need for two extra employees in electronics on Thursday and Friday evenings and the extra staff in the clothing department on Wednesdays. The reasoning behind this may not be clear, but experience will show such customer patterns.

And then there's technology. What does adding three self-checkout stations do for you? How long before you break even on the expense of installing them? What further costs come from maintenance? How does this realign your existing workforce?

Eventually, you end up with a number of variables that can all fluctuate depending on your strategy.

Every supermarket manager is manipulating these variables. Consider the difference between Walmart and Nordstrom. Walmart is all about low cost. They are willing to have longer lines in order to reduce staff and keep prices low. They would also rather you have to walk around an extra three minutes to find an employee in electronics so they can keep their prices as low as possible in that department. Nordstrom, on the other hand, has built its brand around customer service. You will never wait in line at a Nordstrom. But Nordstrom also provides excellent training to make sure their teams are visible but not intrusive—another variable related to customer satisfaction. You don't notice all the Nordstrom employees around until you have a question. Then they're everywhere.

Most businesses make decisions involving these variables without using the math to predict results. They use linear algebra because the stochastic calculus *seems* beyond their capabilities. So those more advanced decisions are run mostly on gut. It seems like electronics is extra busy on Fridays. Maybe we add two more employees and see if that helps the numbers in a few months. It *seems* like the grocery department offers worse customer service, so maybe we should move a couple people from the meat counter that *seems* to do better into that area and see if it boosts sales.

Some managers have great gut instinct and can intuitively make very good decisions in this way. But it's left to innate talent and a certain amount of luck.

But it doesn't have to work that way. The math can model these solutions, allowing for a standardized ability to make workforce decisions. If your turnover is at 20 percent you can model if that is ideal for your profitability. You can model whether it's worth the investment to make changes to get that number down to 15 percent. You can model whether it's worthwhile to open more cash registers or move more people into electronics or the grocery department.

Without having to run a pilot or jump into the deep end with a major shift in strategy, you can put the idea into the computer, and you can see what will happen.

The same math required to model out these possibilities at Walmart or Nordstrom works for IBM, Goldman Sachs, and Boeing. The variables may be different industry to industry. Usually, you'll have a set of variables coming from HR and another set coming from finances—

perhaps around six from each. But once you define those variables and put data behind them, the math can model out demand, supply, and so on across your labor force—no matter the specifics of your business.

This is the math behind the fact that it takes ten minutes to load a Southwest plane and it takes twenty to load a United plane. It's the math behind boarding business-class passengers first even if it slows the process down. It's the math behind how many flight attendants you have on each flight and the decision to hire another ten members of ground crew at the airport.

When you model this out, it comes out in a graph that looks like a fishbone. You can see where the data comes in at various points as the "spine" crawls across the x-axis.

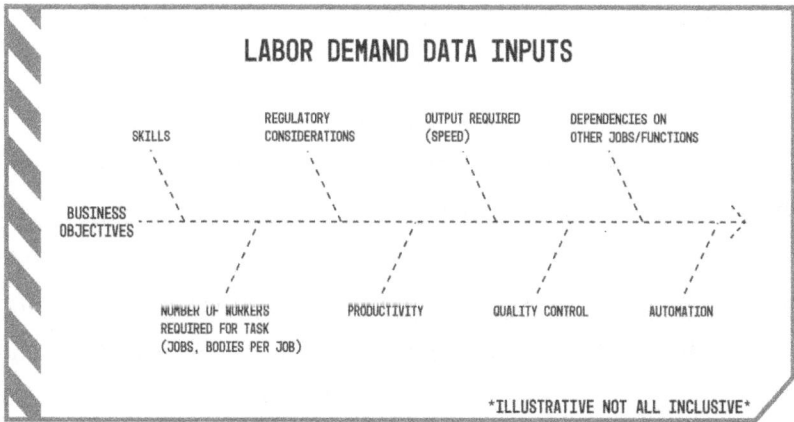

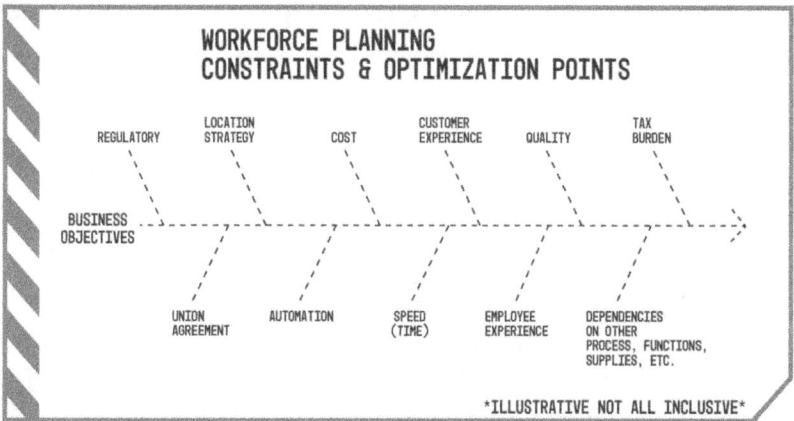

LABOR DEMAND DATA INPUTS

SKILLS	REGULATORY CONSIDERATIONS	OUTPUT REQUIRED (SPEED)	DEPENDENCIES ON OTHER JOBS/FUNCTIONS

BUSINESS OBJECTIVES

NUMBER OF WORKERS REQUIRED FOR TASK (JOBS, BODIES PER JOB)	PRODUCTIVITY	QUALITY CONTROL	AUTOMATION

ILLUSTRATIVE NOT ALL INCLUSIVE

WORKFORCE PLANNING CONSTRAINTS & OPTIMIZATION POINTS

REGULATORY	LOCATION STRATEGY	COST	CUSTOMER EXPERIENCE	QUALITY	TAX BURDEN

BUSINESS OBJECTIVES

UNION AGREEMENT	AUTOMATION	SPEED (TIME)	EMPLOYEE EXPERIENCE	DEPENDENCIES ON OTHER PROCESS, FUNCTIONS, SUPPLIES, ETC.

ILLUSTRATIVE NOT ALL INCLUSIVE

There are immensely complicated formulas behind this, but that, in principle, is what we're doing here. And as a leader of your organization, that's all you need to understand in order to use the models to predict workforce needs.

The Science of Leadership

When it comes to natural forces, we can often stop at the math that models them. However, we can't forget that we're working with people here. For that, we also have to add science.

We call this science industrial psychology. It involves the study of human productivity and human effectiveness. For our purposes, we're looking at how people respond to your corporate organization.

What motivates your people? What drives them? What makes the whole more than the sum of the parts? What allows four scientists to change the world where four other scientists never develop a major marketable solution?

Answers to these questions require scientific insight and human solutions. It also offers a check on some of our math. The model may tell you that you should have ten thousand employees in America and spread the rest over India, Vietnam, and Costa Rica. But the science warns against issues in providing leadership over immense distance and cultural difference. It might also limit interaction across teams or departments.

The math can model how long talent is likely to stay, but it requires industrial science to create an organization that inspires that talent to love their work and stay longer—or to work more effectively.

When we combine the science with the math, though, we have a complete process that can model human behavior and business need.

The Scope of the Challenge

Before we dig into the models, though, we have to come to terms with the complexity of the challenge we face.

Let's start with some pretty basic questions. How do you know how many people you need? How do you know you have the right people in the right positions? How do you replace your "irreplaceable" talent? Does everyone in your organization have the aptitude for the changes that are ahead—even when you don't quite know what those changes will look like?

These are questions every leader has to ask themselves. There have been times when those questions were relatively straightforward to answer. But they've become harder to answer in recent years because of multiple accelerating trends in the economy.

The first of these trends is demographics. As every employer knows, right now, there are more jobs than there are workers in the workforce. And this trend is only going to continue—at least for a while. We're now in the midst of a great generational shift. While it's ten or fifteen years later than everyone predicted it would be, the baby boomers are finally retiring and leaving the workforce, and Generation X is moving into upper-management positions. However, Generation X is small, and Millennials and Gen Z together are only about the size of the baby boomers. In this case, the math is pretty straightforward. We're only just entering an era in which there are more jobs than workers.

This trend is further complicated by the next one. This is the ongoing change in what workers expect from their employers. Ever since Gen X hit the workplace, there's been an increasing skepticism of the employer and increasing demands for better work–life balance. Long gone are the days of workers sticking with one company for their entire career. Organizational scientists will tell you that layoffs that occurred in the 1970s and 1980s in almost every industry broke that trust relationship with employees, and employees have not forgotten. Even today we are seeing a resurgence in the labor movement that still revolves around this trust relationship between employee and employer.

Once that implicit trust workers had in their companies to take care of them was broken, workers pushed back on how and when work was performed. This trend accelerated during the COVID pandemic and through the influx of Millennials and Gen Z into the workplace. This adds extra urgency to the demographic trends because it means there's a ticking clock on those high-level positions the baby boomers are about to free up. Here's what I mean: Baby boomers have extended their careers beyond traditional limits. But Gen Xers, by and large, have a different relationship to work. They don't define themselves by it like the baby boomers do. That means they are likely to retire *on time*—only about a decade after they step into those high-level positions. That does not necessarily provide adequate time for Millennials and Gen Z to gain the experience necessary to fill those leadership roles. This is further complicated by research that says Millennials and Gen Z take this trend even further. With each new generation, it's harder to retain talent and keep them invested.

Relatedly, this is where remote and hybrid work expectations come in. While there's been some reversal in this trend abroad, in America it remains a live issue—at least for now.

All this is occurring while businesses are also wrestling with a trend of moving away from rigid role construction. HR 101 teaches that businesses should organize talent along a ladder. In finance, you begin your career as a junior accountant. After you gain some experience, you climb up to the accountant role. Then, you become an accounting manager, then treasurer, controller, and so on. In tech, the ladder gets split into two: one climbing up into management and the other climbing up through technical skills. But the format is the same.

The ladder approach has been a reliable tool in company organization for decades, but it is quickly becoming outdated. The world we're moving into is one in which employees may hop to various rungs of various ladders across departments in a single company. An analyst may have functions across HR, finance, supply chain, and sales—and the cost center might be divided between all those departments to pay for that job. Careers increasingly look more like neural networks, with talent moving laterally and diagonally, as well as vertically, and sometimes all at the same time.

Next up, we have automation. This is the trend that gets all the press these days. On the extreme end, we have things like ChatGPT and other advanced AI reimagining roles and responsibilities, but this trend also includes machine learning, robotic process automation, and a whole range of technologies where you can develop a decision tree and rely on a computer to complete tasks. This trend has been with us for decades now, but it has seen recent leaps with more advanced capabilities, particularly in regard to text and speech.

Importantly, though, this is not a simple solution for all workforce planning problems, nor is it likely to significantly reduce the size of that workforce or the cost of workers. Instead, this new technology will force roles to evolve and become more technical—as it always does. When the robots came for the assembly-line workers in the 1970s and 1980s, it did reduce the number of workers, but those who remain are extremely well-paid. For instance, Ford's workforce in 1970 was around 225,000. As recently as 2019, it was 190,000. Admittedly, a smaller number, but not quite the complete replacement some expected. There was a period in the early 2000s when Ford had as few as 90,000 workers, but over time, they had to hire back most of those cuts, and often at much higher costs.

This change has within it another mini trend, which is the movement of labor. With muscle labor, the move we've seen over the past few decades was to go where it was cheapest. Manufacturing moved overseas to save costs. There's been some reversion of this since COVID, but it's unlikely to truly reverse in any meaningful way. Instead, it will more likely continue to hop to new destinations as current locations move from low-income countries to medium-income countries. China is already seeing business leave for Vietnam and other Southeast Asian countries. Developments in automation, however, show a different movement: the pooling of businesses around areas where talent collects, whether that's Austin, Silicon Valley, or Miami.

In other words, while companies with physical labor needs will continue to shift from country to country abroad, companies with knowledge labor needs will have to chase those knowledge workers here and meet them where they're at.

Labor is further complicated by our next trend, which is the continual shift to a mixed workforce. Most companies now have a mix of direct labor and indirect labor. Along with your traditional W-2 full-time employees, you have consultants, gig workers, and part-time assistants. Some of these people you work with all year every year, and others you bring in once for two weeks of work on a special project. Every company has to find the right mix for their circumstances.

All of these trends have to be navigated while also considering the standard macroeconomic trends that are always at work. Is the economy growing or shrinking? What are people buying? What are the interest rates this quarter? Are people saving or spending more of their income?

Facing all these competing trends, it's no wonder that businesses find it difficult to predict their workforce needs or manage the workforce talent they have. After all, that's a lot of variables floating around. How are you supposed to account for all of them in your modeling? Adding to this complexity, these trends affect each business and each industry in very unique, specific ways. For instance, automation looks different for McDonald's—which is already moving to fully automated drive-thrus—than it does for UnitedHealth Group or Berkshire Hathaway.

Luckily, technology has come to our aid, making it far easier to collect the data we need to run our models.

Solutions for Every Budget

I recently saw a video reviewing a particular Disney customer service policy. Anyone who has been to a Disney theme park knows that the company puts a high premium on the customer experience. But who do you think they focus their training on to help when a child gets lost?

The first, most obvious person is not an actor or running the rides or in the gift shop. It's actually a member of the custodial staff. There's always someone emptying the garbage cans around the park, and Disney has clearly trained those people to have good customer service skills. The video I watched showed one of the janitors comforting a lost child after radioing to the team so they could find the child's parents. In the video, the janitor took his bottle of water and used it to draw Mickey Mouse ears on the ground so the child wouldn't panic.

If, God forbid, it was ever your child that was lost, you'd remember that janitor and the park that trained them for the rest of your life. That's precisely what Disney aims for—and they have the financial superpower to research, staff, and train for this scenario.

I've seen the power of this firsthand. Many years ago, I went to a party at the Disneyland Hotel with a friend. While we were out on the dance floor at our hotel, someone stole her purse. We didn't even have time to notice it was gone. By the time we got back to our table, a Disney employee was there to tap her on the shoulder, tell her what happened, and ask her to come down and identify the purse.

Disney has been able to manage its workforce at this elite level for years because it is a massive company that prioritizes such planning and management. But these days, you don't have to be a massive company to have this level of data analysis. It's likely Disney spent a significant amount running numbers to discover that their janitors need extra training to help if children get lost. But with advances in AI and machine learning, among other technologies, these insights are available much more quickly and at much smaller budgets.

Moderna was not a huge company when it installed advanced, scientifically backed workforce planning into its organization. Nor was the chemical company working on developing a cure for blindness.

We're living in a new era of capabilities, and one of the most important areas of advancement will be workforce planning. When I was at HP, we ran our workforce planning function through Excel. It took ninety people to run the numbers. We had so many different systems, we had to just dump the data somewhere so we could manipulate it and analyze it. Today, you could do it with fifteen people at the same scale.

Once you understand the ideas behind the science, these solutions become tenable, no matter the size of your company or its industry—allowing you to find the same kind of "simple" solutions that transformed Cencora's warehouses.

CHAPTER 2

Creating Conditions for Success

Walmart is a marvel of modern business. Ranked right at the top of the Fortune 500 list, the company brings in around $600 billion in revenue every year. That success is built on Walmart's incredible workforce planning and talent strategy. While never being the highest payer in its field, and famously union averse, the company somehow manages to keep its more than ten thousand stores across nineteen countries running smoothly. Prices are always low, while operations are streamlined. Such operational efficiency is the envy of the entire business world.

Yet even Walmart's model has certain shortcomings. In particular, the company struggles to implement that same level of efficiency in its corporate functions. Finance, HR, corporate procurement, and technology: Each division is overstaffed and overspends for its production. As stated in their 2022 annual report, they are running overhead at significantly higher than industry average and are looking to reduce that spend to industry norms over the next few years. The gap is significant. Walmart overhead costs are around 15 percent, where, according to the Mercer 2022 Retail Trends Report, the industry average is 10.2 percent.

This team of 130,000 individuals is a cost center for Walmart, and the extra expense impacts performance. And the reason is simple: Walmart doesn't follow the same rules in its office that it sets for its stores. A company that is almost fanatical about cost control in its stores regularly sees massive overruns—particularly in its IT workforce—because it sets aside its famous love of generic alternatives and insists on bespoke technology solutions built in-house.

There are wonderful HR software options out there that Walmart could buy off the shelf and tailor to work across its company. Procter & Gamble has one. It cost them $4 million to deploy globally. Walmart built their own and spent around $20 million—just for North America.

These costs extend beyond just the price of building that software. It creates difficulties for back-office workforce planning across continents. Workforce solutions are limited because the systems in countries like Ireland and Israel are different. The data is structured differently. The data tracked is different, and the systems can't talk to one another, making it extremely difficult to compare and analyze.

Despite all of Walmart's incredible capability in running its stores, the company is still capable of making errors. Those errors have nothing to do with its ability to implement the ideas we'll cover ahead. Instead, it's a matter of failing to set all the right conditions for success. By breaking its own rules, Walmart limits its own capacity for success.

No System Works without the Right Preconditions

Before jumping into the process for creating talent prophecy capacity in your business, I want to take a moment to slow down. There's so much potential in a great workforce planning and talent strategy model, it's easy to assume they will work in an instant and fix everything. Some might assume you can open the box, install the system, and watch as it removes all obstacles in your path. But it doesn't really work like that.

The ideas I'll share can make a radical difference to your business, but they require the right conditions to do so. And if the right understanding isn't already in place with leadership, even a company as successful as Walmart can struggle.

To avoid that struggle, you need to create controls for the condition of the biases within your company. No experiment can be a success if it doesn't have the right controls in place. Controls account for all the factors that can influence results. For instance, if you ran an experiment to see which type of household plant grew fastest, you'd need to control for access to daylight, quality of soil, and the amount of water required. Otherwise, you couldn't really use the results.

The same is true of workforce planning and talent strategy. You need the right controlling concepts in place to use the analysis you will gain. You have to control for biases about results, assumptions about the use of technology, and outside influences that can affect how you understand and use these predictive powers.

If you don't put these controls in place first, nothing that comes after will net nearly as much improvement as you hope.

Trust Your Results

Here's some good news. These systems do *not* require massive investment up front and years of time before you see a return on that investment. Yes, the old adage is true that you have to spend money to make money, but the amounts here are *not* in the tens of millions and do not take years to deploy. However, if you want to realize results, you'll need to trust the models providing you with the answers.

This is the first and most important of your controls. After all, an experiment is worthless if you don't accept the results. If you don't trust the information that your workforce planning model provides you, it can't offer you much support in your decision-making. This is where HP and IBM fell short in past efforts to implement these types of solutions. They had the information they needed at hand, but they chose to ignore it—to disastrous consequences.

I know trusting new analysis can be uncomfortable. It feels unproven, and there's a natural instinct to want to hedge. Think back to the first time you used a GPS to navigate your way around a city you knew well. When it told you to take a route you weren't used to, it's likely you made the natural assumption that the technology didn't know this city as well as you did. It was only after hitting traffic on that trip—or finally trusting it on a later trip and discovering you arrived five minutes faster than normal—that you finally put some trust in the technology.

Nowadays, most of us turn on Google Maps every time we're going somewhere new without any question of whether we'll allow it to guide us. We've come to see that its results, even if at times imperfect, are generally better than trying to get somewhere without it—that the map algorithms and real-time traffic data know things that we cannot and can adjust in real time for those situations. The same is true of good talent management and workforce planning.

If you want to run an evidence-based HR department, you'll have to do the same thing with your workforce planning and talent strategy models. You'll have to trust the results you're receiving. As with your Google Maps app, you don't have to understand all the math and science going into the technology. But you do have to let it guide you.

This is, admittedly, particularly difficult for a department like HR, which is usually filled with individuals with strong interpersonal skills but limited analytical and technological understanding. But you must control for this. The future will require your team to stretch themselves and incorporate more data into their decision-making.

If you can get people on board initially, the results will continue to boost confidence. Just like your realization that you could trust Google Maps, your team will soon learn there's value in trusting your models.

Technology Is an Enabler, Not a Solution

I've touched on the limitations of technology above, but I want to make it explicit here that you have to control for those limitations in your understanding of what these models can achieve. This technology—like all technology—is a powerful enabler of better business practices. What it is not is a one-stop-shop solution for all labor issues.

Technology rarely if ever solves a problem. What it does—with good governance and process—is allow us to scale, optimize, and drive our solutions efficiently.

Business leaders often dream of a future in which technology reduces their need to consider labor at all. Instead of modeling workforce needs, they hope that automation, AI, and other innovations will allow them to resolve all talent gaps or workforce budget issues they have—and do so all at once. Some even seem to hope that technology will replace their entire workforce, removing the need for much prediction at all.

We've been through several waves of major technological break-throughs in the last half century, and the pattern is clear: Technology tends to create *more* jobs and *raise* costs, even as it offers new oppor-tunities to increase revenue and efficiency. The nature of those jobs and costs change, but the technology never offers a magical solution.

The reason for this is simple. Technology enables new possibilities, but it is not a savior. It partners with human beings to provide new capabilities. And the humans working with the technology require more knowledge and skills—and those cost money because they are the qualities every employer is searching for.

Recent technological developments follow this same trend. The more responsibilities we delegate to machines, the more we have to watch over them, because machines cannot interact with the world unsupervised. AI may deliver some impressive results in the coming years, but it isn't hard to find examples of its disastrous failures when left unattended. A few years ago, Microsoft turned on an AI-enabled Twitter bot. It took the bot all of about an hour and a half to become racist and bigoted.

The bot was not racist. It wasn't anything. It was a machine, and it simply fulfilled tasks according to its algorithms. When left alone, it scraped the internet, found all sorts of unsavory material that was popular in the dark corners of social media, and began posting it.

Many people overestimate how "smart" AI and other technology are. The capabilities of our computers are significant, but the term "intelligence" is a misnomer. These are not thinking machines. They do calculations and run on probabilities. And those probabilities have limitations that require human intervention.

If you say something is 94.8 percent likely, a human gets that the opposite will happen a little more than 5 percent of the time—a not insignificant chance. Humans naturally adjust for the rare but possible. We pay all kinds of insurance for such circumstances. And we adjust on the fly when we are confronted with the rare but possible. But a self-driving car that has a 5 percent failure rate when it sees a stop sign cannot adjust for that itself. And it only takes twenty stop signs for it to fail. That's an extreme example, but one that's front-page news every time an accident or death occurs as a result.

A machine will acknowledge this 5 percent exists, but it will always pivot to the majority solution because that's how they work. They don't think or have judgment. Only people do.

Workforce planning and talent strategy are not AI, but the results are impressive enough that it's easy to assume they model their way to anything. The fact is, technology is a valuable partner in workforce predictability, but it is not going to solve issues with talent, budgets, and output in and of itself. It isn't capable of that—no technology is.

To ever reach such a level of capability would require a perfect world with perfect data. That's simply not the world we live in. For instance, I recently saw an AI-generated article on the top ten greatest college football teams of all time. A friend sent it to me because it had the 2003 USC team, my alma mater, in the second spot.

The thing is, great as that team was, it wasn't even in the top three USC teams of all time. But this wasn't the only odd choice. The list was weighted entirely toward the twenty-first century. The only exception was the 1995 Nebraska team.

The reason for this is obvious. The AI scraped articles about great teams from around the web, and all those articles were written in the last twenty years. The AI had no historical knowledge or sense of personal judgment. It was just repeating back the information it was fed. In doing so, it missed the 1946 Army team, and many other examples from different eras in the game. It was Microsoft's Twitter bot all over again.

We as a society create immense amounts of data, and it grows exponentially year over year. However, the computer age is relatively recent, as is the interconnectivity of the web and cloud computing. This creates a natural bias to the most recent when trends tend to develop over time, and human nature, for all our advancements, hasn't changed all that much. In modeling likely behavior, a longer view is needed. And we can only do so much to model that through our algorithms.

The data you feed into your workforce planning and talent strategy models will be similarly faulty. It's impossible to be otherwise. Even with excellent data on every person in your company—knowing all their talents and all the indicators in their lives that would help predict behavior—you'd still see failures to account for individual choices. For instance, you cannot forecast what my reaction will be if I am fortunate enough to win the lottery next week. Do I come into work, or do I quit? If I do come in, do I put in the same amount of effort because I love the job, or do I slack off and keep showing up just to have something to do?

When I worked at Microsoft, I was offered a big promotion. The only problem was I had recently gotten married. Microsoft assumed I'd be happy to take the bigger paycheck, the increase in responsibilities, and move to Seattle. I'm sure many people in my exact position would have done so. But not me. I wasn't going to move with my new wife that soon into our marriage.

Microsoft could not have predicted if I was the sort of person who would move or not based on the data they had. It was an individual, unique characteristic. And computers will never be able to fully model for that—not in AI and not in workforce planning.

All of which is to say that this will not replace all your people. You may find you need a smaller workforce with this. You may find you need a larger one or that the composition of that workforce needs to change. Regardless, it will only become more important that you have the right people in the right positions at the right price and, most importantly, with the right skills in order to adapt to this technology and any other new technology down the line.

Don't Aim for Perfection

This leads to another huge issue you have to control for: the desire for perfection. If data and technology can never be perfect or fully replace the need for human oversight, you'll never achieve perfect accuracy in your talent prophesies.

Procter & Gamble runs its workforce planning extremely well. The company navigates its mixed workforce at an expert level and has incredible predictive powers for changes in that workforce. Their HR Analytics is one of the gold standards out there in the world.

But the company's success rate of those predictions is still around just 80 percent. That means one out of every five predictions the company makes about its talent is going to be wrong. That's OK. Two steps forward and one step back is still one step forward. And the numbers are even better when it's five steps forward and only one back.

A lack of perfection is a fact of life in workforce planning. Simply put, there is science here, but there is also a dark art in forecasting human nature. And that means there will never be 100 percent certainty here. As I said above, no matter how great your system or how elite your data collection, you will never achieve perfection. And waiting for perfection—or something close to it—only harms your decision-making today.

Humans being what they are, we'll never have perfect clarity on individual decisions of individual employees or how individuals will respond to life events. We'll never be completely certain if a financial shift in the market will happen in this quarter or the next one or not at all. So, you won't ever know with 100 percent certitude whether the $2 million you spend will lower turnover from 8 percent to 6 percent—or whether that will be money well spent.

That's something you're just going to have to accept. Otherwise, you'll never have results you can use in your business.

However, this is no reason to put the book down and walk away. The truth is that the data is never perfect and doesn't have to be perfect. The models don't require perfection. All they have to do is tell you, based on all the data available, what's *most likely* to happen. Having the most likely scenario at hand offers profound power to decision-makers. It's equivalent to getting the morning weather report. We all know there are days the meteorologists get it wrong and days we use our best judgment and take the umbrella even if the prediction is for sunshine. But it's still an incredible resource that usually gets its predictions right.

Put another way, 50 percent capability to forecast your future workforce is 50 percent better than what you have today.

And raising your capability 50 percent isn't the end of the road. As we'll see later, workforce planning is a process that involves constant refinement. Every time you make a prediction, you update the system with the results. You train the model to become better.

Once you've installed this system into your business, each iteration will net better levels of predictability. The trick is controlling for expectations of perfection in order to begin the process now—and in driving end users to actually use the results and trust the process even though there are no guaranteed answers.

Accept the Ethics and External Forces

As I've already mentioned, this book is agnostic on certain controversial business practices. I won't come down one way or the other on things like offshoring or the value or drawbacks of unions. Workforce planning and talent management will involve those things, but this is not the space to argue over one strategy or another.

However, I will note here that leaders must recognize that there are ethical complexities—as well as certain external considerations—that may complicate their decision-making. You have to control for the external forces that will always play a part in your decisions.

For instance, your planning may predict significant savings if you offshored two thousand jobs. That is a budgetary decision. But there is also a human cost. Such a change will involve two thousand people you currently employ losing their jobs. There is also a PR cost and a political cost behind those savings. It's not for me to say whether that makes it the right decision or the wrong one, but every leader knows it is a consideration.

That same consideration is present when replacing employees with technology and other potential shifts in strategy.

For instance, Coca-Cola could save money moving its bottling jobs to only low-cost countries abroad, but the company has a culture that prioritizes keeping those jobs in America—as well as in other countries in which they sell product. They have chosen to bottle for the local markets. Leadership has determined that it is the right decision for Coca-Cola whatever its models predict.

In addition to these ethical issues, we must recognize that we live in an era in which such decisions come at a price. Part of the changing workforce expectations I mentioned in the last chapter is the trend of Millennials and Gen Z to hold companies accountable for their actions—and that includes decisions about your workforce. There can be major costs if such decisions are not sold effectively to customers and employees.

You also have to control for things like ESG. Such considerations may or may not make a business more ethical, but the reality is that companies are judged by those standards—judged by employees, customers, and investors. Your predictions may offer enough upside to break certain ESG promises, but that's an individual decision for leadership.

As is opening a factory in Southeast Asia. That choice may make sense using your models, but you will have to decide whether the potential fallout changes that calculation. Is that decision worth a potential customer boycott or some of your higher-level talent choosing to find jobs elsewhere? The models won't be able to make that call for you.

Nor can they decide when there are reasons to settle for alternative arrangements. MetLife took its workforce predictions about moving talent out of New York City. Their aim was to shift their team upstate to Syracuse, where costs were lower. However, they ended up moving some positions not to Syracuse but Charlotte, North Carolina. The loss of certain efficiency and savings was more than made up for by the tax deal Charlotte's local government made with the company.

MetLife split its workforce even though the models would have told the company to keep people together. ExxonMobil paid over what the models would have suggested they had to pay in order to keep teams in valuable locations. They offered employees four times their usual salary to move to Angola during an ongoing civil war. The value of the oil was worth the extra cost and risk—no matter what the models suggested.

Exxon's example is not an outlier. There will always be potential political and geopolitical considerations that fall outside the scope of your modeling. Many companies struggled with workforce decisions in Russia in the wake of the invasion of Ukraine. They had to balance outrage from stakeholders and governments with huge potential upsides capturing cheap, well-educated labor in that country.

In another famous example, Disney reportedly froze new hirings in Florida during its dispute with Governor Ron DeSantis. The company had planned to add two thousand jobs beforehand, but political reality intruded.

Intel manufactures its chips in Taiwan instead of China, where the work could be done more cheaply, because Taiwan is more likely to abide by the strict protocols necessary to ensure the quality of Intel's microchips. China is also famous for requiring factories to be at least 51 percent Chinese owned, allowing them to study the technologies being produced there and replicate them. Those external considerations make the relative expense of working in Taiwan a worthwhile one—for Intel at least.

One final example. During the COVID pandemic, AstraZeneca produced one of the most widely distributed vaccines in the world. The company never even attempted to get approval to use the vaccine in the United States. With the mRNA vaccines already approved and controversies over the Johnson & Johnson vaccine (which was quite similar to AstraZeneca's), it didn't seem worth it. However, that didn't stop the company from producing those vaccines in a factory in Delaware. Nor did it keep the company from opening a factory within the African Union to produce some of its vaccine supply there.

In both cases, there were workforce considerations that trumped modeling. AstraZeneca already had a plant in America. Moving it to another country would be a waste of time and money during an international emergency. However, opening a plant in Africa was the price the company had to pay to open up that market. The benefits clearly outweighed the costs there.

Controlling Prophecy

There's huge value in predictability, but only if we recognize its limitations. Your models will never be 100 percent accurate, but you have to trust them anyway. They will not be able to predict whether a boycott is likely to be painful enough to eat up all your savings after moving jobs abroad or whether a factory in a less desirable location actually offers more upside because it opens up a new market. They won't game out the ethical consequences of replacing five hundred people with AI.

That's where your leadership comes in. However, if you implement these ideas, you'll be in a far better position to make those tough decisions. Imagine having a clear idea of how significant your savings would be or what your increases in productivity might look like when introducing that AI or moving that factory. Imagine knowing the value of keeping a large workforce in China and what it would cost to build a workforce in Vietnam instead.

That predictive clarity makes your choices far clearer. You'll still have to make the call, but you can have confidence you understand the stakes.

That can be your future—so long as you control for biases and outside considerations and implement the complete process.

PART II

THE TALENT PROPHECY PROCESS

CHAPTER 3

Creating Units of Labor

One of the biggest issues companies face is objective comparison of work. How do you compare one employee to another? Or one contractor to another? Or one potential hire to another? This is often an underexamined consideration in business, but it leads to numerous difficulties.

For instance, let's say you need to hire a consultant for advice on a major initiative you're considering. To narrow down your options, you look at the major constancy firms out there—the Deloittes and McKinseys of the world. They both have experts with a lot of experience. They're both good at what they do. And they both have excellent track records.

If both consultancy firms have similarly qualified experts in your area, how do you choose one over the other? How do you compare their potential?

Often, companies make such calls based entirely on gut instinct. They see both presentations and go with the one they felt spoke more toward their ambitions. They might go with the consultant who made the biggest promises or the one who seemed to get into the most detail. Or they might just choose the consultant who held their attention best.

But that doesn't mean they chose the *right* consultant for their needs.

Similarly, companies often struggle to compare one worker to another. This isn't just a business problem; it's an issue the government struggles with all the time. About twenty years ago, the federal government implemented "pay for performance" systems (they attempted this widely in both the DHS and the DoD) that set compensation based on the achievement of individual goals. Each employee was rated on their success in reaching their goals—on a scale of one to three. The idea was to cut costs by limiting bonuses to those who truly excelled in their positions. Unfortunately, the system failed to control costs to achieve better results. Because the goals were individual, the vast majority still earned a number one rating and their bonus. Given the size of the bonus pool was finite, that meant bonus payouts divided among 85 percent instead of 10 percent were basically insignificant as a motivator for higher achievement.

To avoid that trap, many companies instead compare employee production across a department. In this system, if you and I are, say, a level seven in our organization, our performance is meant to be on par. We may or may not have the same skills or jobs, but a level seven is a level seven is a level seven. Results of our output should be roughly equal in our given profession. This is far better than pay for performance, but often, it too has shortcomings. In the first place, it doesn't track our skills. I may have a set of skills that would be extremely valuable in another department, but our company would have no idea. Instead, I might miss out on promotions because my skills put me at the low end of my peer group.

Additionally, companies like to see employee performance fit nicely into a bell curve. Where I fall on that bell curve will determine if I get a promotion or a raise. It'll determine where I am in line when there are cuts in my department.

But creating a bell curve forces individuals to fit a distribution that may or may not match reality. Imagine having a team with four rock stars on it. But you can't recognize all four because that wouldn't map onto the curve. Instead, someone has to be at the bottom and one or two need to be in the middle—even if that doesn't accurately reflect performance.

Those performance ratings can trail some of your top employees for their entire careers at your company. Some may miss out on promotions. Many will choose to leave.

The alternative is also possible. A team full of underperformers will still be forced to chart onto the bell curve even if all should be moved or replaced. Some may end up with the promotions their more deserving colleagues miss out on.

And here, once again, we have no sense of whether the right people with the right skills are in the right positions—or if they could be moved to other positions and work more effectively.

This leaves us back where we started. Who should be promoted? Who should be paid more? Who is a priority to retain? It's the same wall we run into when choosing a consultancy firm.

But it doesn't have to be. There's a better way to measure and compare performance. And that process turns out to be the key to elite workforce planning and talent strategy.

Work at the Skill Level

The key here is to take what we do every day and break it down to the skills and time required to complete it. That will allow us to quantify the demand, your current supply, and available supply elsewhere.

Far too often, companies get caught in the trap of building their understanding of work at the job level. Let's say your organization has three thousand employees. These employees are spread across a number of divisions—finance, sales, procurement, and so on. These divisions are job families. Underneath each job family are the specific jobs these employees hold. In finance, that would include positions like financial analyst, AP clerk, treasurer, etc.

This is organizational science 101. Out of those three thousand employees, you might have three hundred positions that fit into perhaps twelve job families.

So far, so straightforward. And that's why most companies stop there. When they write up job descriptions, they build their conception around the performance of their top talent. This is how the bell curve develops. It's the essence of the individual performance metric as well.

On a certain level, this makes sense. When you're lucky enough to get a unicorn in a position, you want to find a way to get everyone to perform to that level. To do that, you rewrite job requirements to match that person's unique skills and capabilities. But in practice you end up with all the issues I've already pointed out—plus an additional headache when you try to measure demand or increase supply in that position.

You simply can't model for unicorns.

Instead, you should build up talent by digging deeper than the job level and concentrating on skills. Here's what I mean. Return to your organizational charts. Under each job, list the set of skills required for each position. For instance, to be a finance manager at your company, a candidate may need three years of experience, a bachelor's degree in business, accounting, or economics, and nine or so particular skills. These skills would typically include experience with general ledger, work with A/P and A/R, MS Excel, financial analysis, etc. Instead of building job descriptions around elite performance, you can build them around these skills. And all your metrics can track how an employee uses those skills in their position.

This makes it far easier to model your current talent and find new talent. It also has several additional benefits. First, it removes the risk of discrimination—at least at the point of hiring and performance measurement. If you are hiring for the best individual person, you are dealing with a lot of subjective choices that may be influenced by biases. If you hire at the skill level, you are modeling what you need and finding those who best exemplify those skills—no matter what they look like or where they come from.

Your decisions are based on what objective needs you have for the position, department, division, and company.

Another benefit is that this makes it easier to see gaps and opportunities within your organization. A finance manager with only seven of those skills clearly needs further training. On the other hand, a finance manager with all nine skills may also possess two skills that are needed elsewhere in another position in that division. When you see the job that way, you can split that employee across the two positions. Perhaps they work thirty hours as a finance manager and ten in the other position. So long as they are paid for their work, they won't mind having their time divided that way. If anything, research shows us the majority embrace the challenge and view it as a company investing in their growth. Out of that view come loyalty and an increase in retention.

You can further adjust hiring and talent retention to prioritize those with the best mix of skills. And you can see who has the skills to adjust to technology changes. If you know the specific skills and experience necessary at the job level, when a machine can replicate one of those skills, you know where to integrate it. It's easier to model what the human interaction with that machine will look like. And you have a better sense of how the job and the tasks associated with it evolve.

The job itself still fits in a position in its job family. However many employees you need, they'll fit in those same jobs—even if the jobs now require different skills and experience.

Finally, organizing your new workforce planning and talent strategy at the job level allows you to optimize performance review and the difficult tasks of bonuses, promotion, and staff reductions that come with it.

By refocusing on measuring at the skill level, you can grade performance using metrics that measure production and the use of the skills associated with that job. Using these metrics, you have a far better idea of who needs training, who deserves a promotion, and who is the priority to retain if there's any downsizing. As the skills of the job evolve, you adjust metrics to judge employees by the new standards.

Suddenly, it becomes much easier to compare talent already in the job. There is no need for subjective self-evaluation or forcing talent to fit into a bell curve. Measurement is objective and fair. If you have four rock stars, all can shine at the same time. If your entire team lacks the necessary skills to perform, that will be clear at the next performance review.

Reducing Work to Units

In order to implement the workforce planning process that follows, you have to take that concept of work at the skill level and translate all the production done through those jobs into units of labor.

It is no exaggeration to say that this is *the* key concept of the book. Nothing is possible without it. I promised not to get too deeply into the weeds with the math in this book, but I'm sure we all remember in chemistry or physics how you need to convert everything in your data to have the same units of measurement. It's difficult to work in inches and centimeters at the same time, and it's impossible to compare tablespoons to degrees Kelvin.

The way around this in workforce planning is units of labor. Until you have a set of units you can use to compare demand and supply to find the gap, you won't be able to prophesy changes to your workforce. Unfortunately, this is not the most natural concept in business leadership. So, let's take it slowly.

Essentially, everything a worker—human or machine—does for your business can be reduced to a standardized unit of labor. Their work can be translated into units of labor. These units break down the work being performed into a combination of the skills required to complete a task and the time required to complete it.

Sometimes, this relationship is very clear. In a factory, each employee might be expected to install a windshield every three minutes. Your unit might then be equal to a single installation or perhaps the number of installations in an hour.

Most work isn't quite that neatly broken down, but it's still possible. Consider the HR task of investigating a sexual harassment claim. If you set your unit at forty hours of work using the skills required to handle those claims, you can break down how many units a standard claim requires.

One unit might go to reviewing the evidence and comparing it to past cases, another to conducting interviews. It might take one unit for it to be reviewed by legal and another to produce a recommendation and for the director to make a decision. Then, you might need another fifteen hours, or about 0.3 units, for HR to review the case.

In total, then, each case takes about 2.3 units. That case may take several weeks and touch several people in several departments, but we can use those units to describe your current and future need, as well as your team's ability to handle that need.

The question then becomes, Do you have sufficient resources, with sufficient skills, to do the work that needs to be done?

Every organization will have many different units of labor—one for every type of work being done—but the key thing is to be able to break each task into a unit so it can be compared across your workforce.

With units of labor, it becomes easier to answer questions like "What's the difference between a senior accountant and a controller that you need one of the latter and seven of the former?"

Once you have your units, you can go back later and both label and model whether the unit is completed by an employee, contractor, or machine.

As I've said, this is a very unnatural step for most managers. But it is also perhaps the most powerful tool in the book. If you do nothing else but implement a system that can measure units of labor, you could easily forecast demand and understand supply. And that is going to improve your organization by 20–30 percent. Simply by creating units of labor, you could run the system on gut instinct and be far more accurate when implementing talent resources. Of course, you'll get better results through systemizing the whole process, but once you have your units of labor, the rest will follow. You'll have the language and the key piece of data you need to understand past projects and forecast future need.

Talent Is a Supply Issue

The chief question of workforce planning is how to take your team and use it in a way that is most productive for the company and the individual members of that team. The first step to that is to build units of labor that can help measure current production across the skills linked to each individual job. The rest of the system is built off our second key insight of this chapter: Labor is like any other supply chain issue. Just like supply chains, labor needs of all sorts follow the same basic formula:

$$\text{Demand} +/- \text{Supply} = \text{Gap}$$

Once you measure the gap, there are different ways you can fill it. And there are ways to reduce demand by improving the supply you already have. Essentially, that's the rest of the process that we'll cover in the chapters ahead.

Some of these processes are very simple—such as gap—and others, like demand and talent management, are more complex. But the overall concept should be familiar to you.

And it's familiar because your company already follows this process to cover these needs within the organization. The problem is that the process is run not by design but by default in most cases. If asked to produce detailed process diagrams of what is done, by whom, and when, most companies cannot. Whatever process you have likely has limited connection to your available data and lacks testable predictability.

Because you're going to learn to use muscles you've never used before, this process will be a challenge at times. But it also pays off quickly. Once you have a standardized process, there's a clear path to mastering it. And once you master it, the benefits are almost immediate—usually inside of thirty to forty-five days.

By day thirty, you'll be able to forecast whether you need five people on a project or six, and where you'll get that sixth person if you need them. And eventually, you'll be able to scale that understanding across your entire organization.

CHAPTER 4

Forecasting Demand

These days, no matter where you are in America, it seems like you can't go more than a mile without tripping over a Starbucks. Sometimes, they're across the street from each other. There's one strip mall in my area with two within three shops.

Despite their close proximity, these Starbucks all act independently. They might share a district manager, but each shop has its own P/L and its own employees.

For years, despite its near saturation, this system worked well for Starbucks—as you could probably tell by the fact even more Starbucks kept opening. But when the pandemic hit, Starbucks, like most companies, had to rethink its strategy. Suddenly, the company had to ramp down its operations when ramping down had never been part of the natural skill set of the company's leaders.

Those leaders suddenly found themselves in a very difficult situation. They wanted to keep as many stores open as possible and lay off as few people as possible. At the same time, they'd have to reckon with longer lines due to fewer stores and social distancing requirements while hoping to maintain typical Starbucks efficiency. Finally, they knew demand for their product would drop as people hunkered down at home, but they would have to adjust in real time to how much sales fell off while figuring out which stores could still be operated profitably in the short term. And of course, the other reality was they would still have leases and equipment costs even if they temporarily shuttered the stores.

There were further complications on the labor side. During the pandemic, there was always a risk that an employee would get ill and would have to self-isolate for weeks. It was fairly common for several employees to get sick at once. And with government stimulus checks and more generous unemployment, many employees didn't want to take the risk of coming in at all.

How was Starbucks going to find enough staff to handle the demand?

Traditionally, the labor side of this ramp-down would have been a combination of limited data and gut instinct. But Starbucks had more powerful tools at their disposal. They developed a unit of labor—coffee sales per hour—to measure the needs at each store that remained open. They took this unit and divided it by the number of in-store employees necessary to keep the coffee flowing. They broke down in great detail every step from taking the order through every node of how the cup was delivered to the customer. For every so many cups of coffee, they knew they needed to add another employee on the shift.

To ensure they had enough people available, they abandoned their old strategy tying employees to one position at one store. Why not, their thinking went, allow employees who usually work at one store to occasionally take a shift at another? So long as the stores were relatively close, it wouldn't make much difference to the employee, but it would allow Starbucks to fill an important shift. If Starbucks had two stores that were less than five minutes' walk from one another, and a barista called out sick with COVID (and potentially their backups had been exposed as well), why not take a trained barista from the other store and ask them to walk over and cover the shift without any undue hardship on anyone?

They also explored cross-training. There's value in specializing, but cross-training team members would add a layer of resilience while labor was tight. It didn't take much time to train a barista on the register or to show the person on register how to warm up and package food. With everyone capable of handling multiple jobs, Starbucks increased their options.

From there, it was relatively straightforward. The company transitioned to running its stores at the district level. Charting each store's coffee sales per hour and projecting them forward, it became increasingly easy to predict demand and therefore the number of employees who had to be scheduled each shift. The company further kept track of the time per order to make sure it still fell within their standards.

It was a massive success, but in short order, the company had a new challenge. The pandemic receded, and suddenly, Starbucks had to ramp its stores back up. All the formerly closed stores would reopen. All the employees who had been sick or didn't want to work were ready to get back to it.

Now, the company had to scale quickly while still maintaining its customer experience. But the same tools that had allowed it to ramp down allowed it to ramp up again.

The benefits to this strategy were numerous. The company remained profitable and successful through an incredibly turbulent period, while also providing its people with the ability to do their job well and remain happy and healthy in their work.

The Value of Forecasting Demand

How many nurses do you need in a hospital on any particular shift? To know that you have to know how many surgical operating rooms you have and how many nurses you need in each operating room. But even that is too simplistic. Some surgeries require more nurses than others. Some require nurses with certain specializations. And of course, that is not all that nurses do.

For all its complexity, hospitals have all the data they need to schedule nurses efficiently to meet their demands. But most don't do it.

New York Presbyterian is the outlier. They have elite command of their demand for nurses across their system, but even they didn't start out aiming for that result. Their initial aim was to increase the time nurses spent nursing. They suspected they could reduce paperwork and bureaucracy to give them more time with patients.

For instance, traditionally, the hospital had assigned one nurse to each surgery whose sole job was to take down notes. Replacing the nurse with another worker was out of the question because New York law stated only doctors and nurses could be in the operating room. But why not use a microphone and AI to transcribe what happened instead of wasting a nurse's shift?

New York Presbyterian wanted to see what that change would look like in practice. Leadership only incidentally stumbled upon an even more impactful lesson. At some point, someone realized that they had thirteen hospitals within a few miles and a few subway stops of one another. Couldn't they shift nurses across the entire hospital system to deal with surges in demand?

If one hospital had a huge number of elective surgeries in a given week, why not ask a few nurses who primarily worked at other hospitals in the area to get off two stops later on the subway and help where the demand was higher? If there was a fire in a particular area of the city, how much effort did it take to get some nurses to switch to that location to provide extra support?

While I have oversimplified for illustrative purposes, these examples are obvious when you state them so boldly, but the real value New York Presbyterian discovered was that its data allowed it to model out those demands into the future.

They already knew instinctively there were more elective surgeries at the beginning of the week and that emergency rooms were busier on the weekends, for example. Just pulling that data forward allowed for modeling of shifts and optimizing of labor deployments.

Such modeling can be a huge boon for both employer and employee. Employers can save on labor and increase efficiency across their entire business. New York Presbyterian may not have to hire as many nurses simply because they can use their models to schedule nurses where they could do the most good.

But this is also good for the nurses. After all, there's a nurse shortage. They were overworked, and far too much of their time was being wasted on paperwork and slow shifts. With better modeling, those nurses will get to do more of what they were trained to do. And getting the chance to do good work is important to people.

The same is true of those cross-trained Starbucks employees. They can grow and be challenged in their work, ultimately advancing their careers by doing the work they are best trained to do. It allows them to be utilized how they want to be utilized and do more of what they want to do. And that makes people happier. Ask anyone working in food service, and it's always better to be busy and have something to do than stand around for hours feeling like a waste.

Feeling better about your work makes you happier. It gives you a better mindset, which makes work a better experience—and that leads to better-quality work, which increases the likelihood of promotions and raises. It's a virtuous cycle that benefits everyone.

When forecasting demand, we're able to determine what skills are necessary and how best to acquire them. Do we retrain the current team or hire for those skills? Do we have people in adjacent jobs that have similar skills that we can move over to the team?

Once you get a handle on demand, you can determine how many people have level-two agile thinking and how many you need with level-four agile thinking. With the demand clear, it's far easier to make the right decision in how to close that gap. With clear numbers, all you have to do is model the costs of various solutions and choose the best one.

Types of Demand

To forecast demand and net all these benefits, you have to recognize that labor demand is a process problem. There is a methodology to how you forecast labor units.

Before we get to the forecast, though, we have to consider the two types of demand. As I alluded to in the last chapter, all work is done in one of two ways: project based or volumetrically. Project-based work is like the work you see on assembly lines. A leads to B to C to D to completion. This type of work is easier to break into labor units. After all, a good project manager should be able to break every project into the blocks to complete a product. Management at a car factory should know how many minutes it takes to assemble each piece of an automobile and to put all the pieces together. One unit might be the three minutes required to attach a windshield. Another might be the one and a half minutes it takes for the machine to create the right door panel.

But this type of work only makes up about 15 percent of the work done in the world. The rest is volumetric. This is most likely the work you're acquainted with in your office. Consider your HR department. As we've already seen, we can still break this work down into units based on the tasks done, the skills required, and the time to complete the task. But the work of people processing Leaves of Absence (LOAs), Benefits Analysis, Labor Relations, or even Recruiting and Employee Development goes up and down. They are not the same week to week, and certain external events control how much work has to be done. An individual might have fifty tasks their job requires but only fifteen that are common while the rest are as needed. But the as-needed tasks can still be forecast and predicted in volume, and therefore, the number of trained professionals necessary determined.

Once you have your units here, you can use simple math to look at all the tasks done by each position and how much your company has to complete those tasks. That's the number of people you need in each position. Eventually, you'll be able to get some general numbers for each job. Perhaps your average HR generalist might look after 350 employees. Once you have 700 employees, you need a second generalist. At 1,150 employees, you need a third. But now you might instead specialize—perhaps bringing in a recruiter instead—who can handle more of a specific task.

The aim is to discover how many units you require for each task and how many units you currently have. No matter your field, you can plot figures along the same lines as your HR hire. At x number of units, you need a new person.

How to Describe Demand

With this information, you can create benchmarks for each position. Remember, we're measuring by the job, not the individual. If the individual can do more than the job, you can move that excess skill or time elsewhere, just as the nurses and baristas shifted locations. That is labor optimization in your talent strategy, and it's important, but also isn't the true gold mine of workforce planning. The main function we're focusing on is modeling volume of work to be performed in order to determine staff size and skills.

These benchmarks can shift over time. For instance, ten years ago, a really good HR department would have one HR employee for every 150 or so employees. Today it's one for every 400 because so much more can be done through automation and self-service (and this has occurred with an actual increase in positive customer experience). Employee information can be updated by the employee and integrated into the system without anyone in HR lifting a finger.

Essentially, machines can be assigned many of the units of labor that used to be handled by workers. Those units have adjusted (becoming smaller as the work is done more quickly) and the skills have changed for HR, but the same system can still describe this change in demand.

You can also adjust demand by your company culture.

When I worked at Microsoft, the company siloed each business unit from the others. So, you had a division for Word and a division for Excel, and the overall business unit they sat in was MS Office. There was a Windows OS division, an Xbox division, and so on. Microsoft took this separation very seriously. They literally had a separate building for Word, a separate building for Excel, and a separate building for PowerPoint.

That's fine, and as we'll see later, Apple has a similarly federated system. But here's where Microsoft is interesting. Org design 101 would tell you that regardless of whether divisions are centralized or federated, you should have one finance function and one HR function across the whole company. You don't need to have a separate function for Word and Excel. The benchmarks for finance and HR in the tech industry would assume this strategy was in place.

However, that wasn't how Microsoft chose to run its business at that point in time. They wanted finance, HR, and procurement to follow common processes and tools, but for each department to be imbedded within each silo. They believed strongly enough in this that they were willing to raise their benchmarks for those positions around 30 percent to cover all the extra demand for staff.

The company culture insisted that everything revolve around the programmers. Bill Gates and co wanted the programmers to have direct access to the people that made the decisions—the people who affected their ability to program—because they felt it made more effective programmers and ultimately better products.

With these benchmarks adjusted, you should now have a general sense of how many people you need in each position and a sense of when to add more to that position. If you need 175 people in sales based on current business levels, you should be able to tell when you have to add the 176th as business picks up.

Build a Model

If you just want to keep doing what you're doing, you could write a workforce plan at this point. With units of labor in place and benchmarks for every position, you could maintain your current course and adjust where needed. But you don't want to just keep doing what you're doing. You want to grow, increase efficiency, and generally improve operations for the business and the workers in it. You want to produce results faster and more cheaply while giving your people meaningful work and room to advance.

To do all that, though, you have to start building models. Models offer you the prophetic powers you're looking for. Instead of just showing where you were or where you are in each position, models will give you the ability to see how changes would affect those jobs and their benchmarks.

What happens when you implement a new AI application into your finance department? What happens if you bring in a dozen new salespeople? How much do your benchmarks shift if you take your employees in data analysis with sales skills and share them across your tech and sales divisions?

When you build your models right, they won't just provide an easy answer; they can show you the ancillary impact on each position.

For instance, think about the McDonald's kiosks that are becoming ever-present in their restaurants. Let's imagine McDonald's has run some pilots, and they've discovered that about 50 percent of customers will use those screens. The obvious impact is that they need 50 percent fewer cashiers. After all, only half their customers are coming up to the register to order anymore.

You don't need a model to understand that. But take a step back. How does this affect the workforce in the back? Before, the vast majority of customers ordered straight off the menu. There was too much risk of the person at the register getting custom changes incorrect. The new screens, though, make it far easier to customize. It's right on the screen, and there's no risk a busy cashier will mishear you.

Now, your orders are more complicated than before, with people not just ordering a Big Mac, but some ordering with double pickles and others with ketchup instead of the special sauce. That's going to slow down the assembly of each Big Mac, and that's going to require more people making the food to avoid delays in delivering the food.

You want your model to be able to tell you whether such a change still benefits your company. Does it still save on labor? Does it speed up orders or slow them down? This used to be something you could only figure out by testing it. Soon, your model should be able to predict those results for you.

CHAPTER 5

Supply

A large telecom company called me in when they were looking to improve their organizational design. As part of a broader effort to compete in the market and adjust talent to changes in technology and the industry, they wanted to simplify the job structure in their networking group—essentially, the engineers who built their systems—along with all their support units. Leadership suspected some redundancy, but they needed a process to truly know one way or the other.

We used software and AI to review their team at the skills level and cataloged the supply of their existing capabilities. As leadership had hoped, we found that they often had positions with different titles and different responsibilities that required the same skills at the same level of expertise. For instance, they had the position of network engineer 1 and system engineer 2, but the difference between the two jobs wasn't at the skill level, it was in the application of those skills. In other words, experience was the main differentiation, and those workers should have been classified the same way.

These discoveries weren't limited to positions that were already in close alignment; they occurred across the entire networking group. Some jobs sat in vastly different places in the company, but the skills necessary were mostly aligned. In our review, we found that those tasked with reviewing vendors had skills not drastically different from those reviewing financial statements.

What the company ended up with was far more clarity on the supply of talent within their organization. They had a better sense of the overall numbers for various crucial skills. For this company, the aim was to just use this information to add more efficiency to their org design. But this same process—and the same information—essentially gives you the supply data you need to compare with your demand.

Comparing Numbers

The basics of supply are simple. Your workforce is capable of doing x. You want to do y. In the last chapter we measured what you need in order to achieve y. Now, the question is the value of x. This is the skill supply you have available.

Once you have this number, you can subtract it from your demand to find the gap in your capabilities and consider your options for filling it, all of which we'll cover in the next chapter. However, in order for this arithmetic to work, you have to be able to compare the numbers of demand and supply—and that means you must stay at the same level of depth for both. If you are working at the job level, stick with the job level. If you're at the skill level for demand, you need to be at the skill level for supply. Essentially, measuring supply has to be in the same language as demand.

As I've said before, the further down you get, the more accuracy and higher efficacy your workforce planning and talent management will have. But if you can only reach the job level on demand, you should stay at that level on supply, even if you are capable of going deeper.

Within this basic point, there is a secondary concern: how important is it for you to get to y? Getting data for supply will cost some money, and it's only worth the time and effort if this is a priority you believe in.

One of the things good workforce planning allows leadership to do is to say our business strategy is to compete with y. However, if getting to y will cost more (or detract too much from other operations in the company) than the benefit it will provide, perhaps the answer is not in your talent management but in your business strategy.

This is an obvious point and may seem simple in concept, but there is cost and complexity here. You have the demand information, but you'll have to make choices on when it is worthwhile to get that same supply data.

When we talk about the supply, the issue is less about whether you *can* get the skills data and more about *how much* you want to get. This is why we really have to consider cost here. Demand is usually more costly, but it's easier to waste money going too deeply into supply. It's absolutely possible to spend $10 million getting skill-level supply data. You can create and maintain complex competency libraries and skills catalogs on a job and employee basis if that is what you wish to do, but that's far more investment than you need to make in order to make most workforce decisions.

Leaders, then, need to prioritize their supply data needs and focus on spending where it makes the most impact. Jack Welch, the former CEO of GE, used to say that if GE couldn't be number one or number two in the market, there was no point in even trying. I'm not saying that's the right philosophy for your company, but it's the kind of philosophy you have to develop when digging into supply.

Before you invest in supply data collection to do y, ask how y is going to make that investment worthwhile. Will you do y better than anyone else? Will you do it more cheaply or quickly? Will you reinvent y in some way?

I know these are fundamental business strategy questions, but don't let them get lost in the discussion simply because y is now more possible with workforce planning. Make sure your business strategy has decided you need y before you use your prophetic powers to get you there from x.

The good news is that once you have data on supply for x, it's much cheaper to update that information. The cost is in the initial effort. Once you know that initial effort justifies gathering all those numbers, it can provide new clarity for years to come.

Buckets of Competencies

Now that you know you need the supply data for x, it's time to look at the various skills you're going to measure for supply. In general, you can break skills into three buckets of competencies.

The first bucket is filled with core skills. These are the skills that all employees have to have—no matter what job they have at your company. These skills can be unique to a company, but some of them are fairly universal. For instance, one core skill might be efficient use of the Microsoft Office suite of programs. Almost every company with an office and computers shares that core skill. Similarly, general communication skills fit here. An employee might be a total introvert, but they still have to be able to communicate with people in meetings and through email.

After the core skills bucket comes the bucket for technical skills. These are the skills required for a specific job. They may exist in multiple jobs, but they're crucial to the particular job or job family you're reviewing. For a programmer, that would probably include fluency in certain coding languages. For management, it could include the ability to deliver bad news.

Some of these skills can range from quite basic—almost core skills—to very complex and refined. For instance, a marketing specialist would need the basic skills of correct spelling and grammar. But they also have to be able to communicate a whole story in a compelling way in under twenty words.

In the final bucket, we have a group of skills related to leadership. These are often more nebulous than core skills around management, which are more technical in nature. You can train someone in how to run a meeting, the structures around having a difficult conversation, or understanding a profit and loss statement—those are technical management skills. Leadership skills, on the other hand, are often harder to teach or quantify. A good leader has passion for the business. They have charisma and gravitas. They can get people to buy into an idea.

It's likely that any demand you have to achieve y is going to require skills from each of these buckets. The value of these buckets, though, is in adjusting your measurement tools as you collect data on your supply.

Assessing Supply Skills

As you lay out the various skills you are measuring for your supply, you'll want to develop a rating system. This rating system should apply to all the skills you need to measure for supply. Despite the more complex nature of leadership skills, they, like all others, can be rated. Many of these skills might be placed in a binary yes/no—either a worker has it or they don't. Checking a box might also apply to certain core skills. Many technical skills, on the other hand, fit on a scale of 1 to 5 or receive a grade from A to F. Be sure to be consistent with ratings. If you use a 1-to-5 scale, stick with that system wherever possible. You also need to be sure you are aligned on what are "nice to have" versus what are "required" skills.

With a rating system in place, you can begin to scan your company for the various skills you want to rate.

Luckily, this process has evolved immensely in the last couple decades. There was a time when there were only two ways to assess skills: self-assessment and management assessment. Self-assessment involved each person naming their experience and listing their skills.

This system had all kinds of problems. In particular, it created incentives for people to try to game it. Usually, they would do this in one of two ways. If they were looking to get a job or earn a promotion, they would overestimate their skills. Someone who had taken a couple semesters of Japanese in college would claim to be fluent. A developer who had just bought a book on Perl would claim they could code an entire website. The other way to game the system would be to underestimate skills. This could lead to increased training opportunities. For that coder who was learning Perl, it might make sense to purposefully say they're weak in it if it could get their company to train them up without any personal cost.

With those shortcomings in mind, companies have sometimes preferred to rely on managers to assess talent. But this system also had issues. Manager assessment was often somewhat subjective and limited. It was based on the material they had seen. An employee might do a particularly poor job on one project but still possess the right skills. Perhaps the issue wasn't the skills but a personal problem or the team leader. How could a manager know one way or the other?

Additionally, with managers often having large teams, it wasn't always possible to have a good sense of all the skills each employee had. Along the same lines, a manager can only judge the skills they see in the job. Imagine one of those software developers was also fluent in Spanish. That might never come up at work. But if their company was planning to open an office in Argentina and needed someone to help train up the new staff, it would be nice to know about that.

The solution many companies have come up with is to have employees assess and managers evaluate. The employees name their skills and their level of competency, and managers verify.

That's fine, and there's no reason to remove those systems if you have them in place already, but we're now in a whole new world of supply data for skills.

With machine learning and AI, we can crawl the web for what employees have already shared with the world in regard to their skills. LinkedIn, Indeed profiles, published papers and projects—there's a lot of information people put out in the world about what they can do. If you had that information, you'd have a far better sense of what skills each person can supply your company.

For instance, if you set AI to scan everything about me online, you'd discover that in the past I used a Chinese honorific. I used it during the time I was living and working in China. It was important to my employer, so anything I put online during that period included that title.

That's the sort of information I'd never think to include in a self-assessment and the sort that a manager would never find in reviewing my work. But if a company discovered that, they'd know I had some connection to China. They'd know I had at least a passing under-standing of certain Chinese customs. They could assume I'd likely spent some time in China on business. Possibly, I might be fluent in Mandarin (unfortunately, I'm not). With that small clue, they could dig a little deeper to discover how advanced my skills might be in this area.

Similarly, in some highly technical fields, vendors have developed assessment software that either through a traditional quiz structure or through a simulation-based question-and-answer model assesses skill proficiency. These are much more accurate but also both expensive and time-consuming for employees to complete. They have benefits and should not be discounted, but they should be used only where benefit can be gained, as the objective here is to move with speed and scale at low cost and to be as unobtrusive as possible.

This new layer of data often gives you room to unearth such powerful insights. For instance, you can often make some educated assumptions about skills based on other skills they make public. So if someone is a database administrator, whether it says on their resume or not that they've done data modeling, you can be pretty sure they also possess that skill. That's usually a job they had earlier in their career.

The same is true for a general ledger accountant. They may not say that they know how to do accounts payable or accounts receivable, but they almost certainly do. Knowing that changes the numbers on supply for that skill in your company.

You can get all this information using machine learning algorithms and basic intelligence decision trees. You can even refine this based on information about performance, how long someone has been in a role, and how many times they hopped from one company to another. All of this helps build a profile of skills available in supply.

Overall, this process is cheap, fast, and unintrusive. Just use computers to review what people have chosen to put out online. Then you can measure their competency with those skills using your new rating system.

This process works particularly well for core skills and those specific technical skills you need in positions. For those more amorphous skills in the third bucket, such as those you find in leadership or that show compatibility in a team, you have to get a little outside the standard box for how you collect data.

For this kind of skills data, you might need to turn to personality and aptitude tests. Myers-Briggs is a famous example. That test has its limits, but it is still a useful tool—and it is by no means the only one out there.

These tests can help nuance your supply. You may have six people with the right technical skills, but do they work well together? Is there a natural leader in that group? Is there someone who always makes sure the numbers are right? Do you have someone with the kind of personality to keep meetings friendly and build bonds? Does someone have the emotional skill set to calm tempers?

You don't want to build a team of yes men just because they have the right technical skills. You don't want your supply filled with people who hate each other. You need people that are going to be able to get along to achieve a common goal.

Data Headaches

When you combine your new data set on technical and core skills with personality tests gauging those less easily quantified skills, you have a pretty good sense of your current supply.

Of course, nothing is ever quite that simple. In collecting this data, you run into three major headaches: accessing data, storing data, and getting the data to "talk" to each other.

The first headache involves the limitations that come from collecting this kind of data. In America, this can often be much easier because we have an "opt out" legal system. However, if you are hiring in Europe, you'll run into the "opt in" limits of data collection. Essentially, in the European Union, each person has to opt into allowing you to scan their online information. That makes this process not impossible but certainly more cumbersome.

Even in the United States, you will run into certain limits. When it comes to scraping available data, you can do that for anyone—you just have to store the data separately from where you keep private information about your direct employees (which we'll cover more in a moment). However, you can't force gig workers or contingent workers to take personality tests. They can choose to take them if asked, but you can't legally require it. There are workarounds here—perhaps trading the test for some training—but it does require a workaround.

If that wasn't enough, you also run into potential data storage issues. Once again, if you're a strictly American company, this isn't too difficult. Any good HR department should be able to store the data securely on your servers. But if your company is international, you'll run into more issues here. Once again, the EU adds an extra layer of protection. It requires all the data you collect on its citizens to be stored in Europe or in a country with similar levels of protection. That's fine if your base is in America, but if you're a Brazilian company, you'll need to store it either in Europe or in a country the EU deems a safe harbor.

And it's worth keeping in mind that these are the laws in place now. It's entirely possible more restrictions will be put in place in the near future.

Even once you jump through all these hoops, there will still be the general concerns about the infrastructure of your servers and the responsibilities this puts on your IT department. These aren't major issues, but they will take up some time and cost.

Once you do have all your data collected and stored, you encounter the final headache. Because you can now gather data from so many sources, you'll end up with a jumble of data coming from

HR, procurement, and finance, as well as external market data. All of this data needs to be able to talk to each other.

Basically, you need an electronic data interface that places all this data in the same language, all at the same skill level you set for demand.

This is not an insurmountable problem, but it is a couple of weeks' worth of labor. Luckily, as with creating the infrastructure to collect supply data, once it exists, it exists. It requires minimal upkeep.

And once all that data is in the same interface and speaking the same language, you can do all your comparisons and all your workforce planning.

Don't Overthink It

I know at this point that this might seem quite complicated. So take a moment to take a breath. Supply is easier than it seems. It's important to remember our controls in chapter 2—in particular, the fact that workforce planning data will never be perfect.

You will never know everything about your supply. You'll never know everything about your employees, let alone all the contractors you work with. But you don't need to know everything. You probably need a good sense of the supply of about eight skills for each job. You won't ever get 100 percent clarity on this, but you don't need it. You want to get as close to an accurate sense of the supply out there as you can.

That way, you can compare it to your demand and have confidence in the gap you arrive at. And once you know the gap, you can look at how you fill it.

CHAPTER 6

Filling the Gap

Cummins designs and manufactures engines and generators. The company has been around for more than a century, and over that time, it's focused primarily on diesel engines. But recently, the company has begun to pivot. They're switching to newer, cleaner alternatives. They aren't going the direction of the car manufacturers with EV battery engines because those won't work on the industrial level Cummins engines often have to. Cummins engines are used in cruise ships, and you aren't going to build a battery big enough to get one of those moving in the middle of the ocean. They are also used in construction zones on industrial sites in the North Sea where you can't drag electrical cords. They need to stand alone.

So what does that mean from a strategy perspective? A simple look at their annual report will show that their best course forward is to switch to hydrogen. They know this transition will take them between ten and fifteen years, and they've been aggressively aiming for that target. They've been buying companies and technology for hydrogen.

But they've run into a problem. There's a deficit of workers who have the skills to manufacture hydrogen engines. In other words, they have a large demand for workers, but the supply is limited. Not enough people are trained up in the technology yet. If Cummins wants to remain at the top of the market, they need to fill that gap between their demand and the supply available on the market.

Because this is new technology, they can't just go out and hire more people. Those people don't exist yet. So Cummins only has one choice, really. They'll have to create the supply themselves through training.

Case closed—but not quite. Cummins is also facing a secondary, longer-term gap in their labor force. They're still building diesel engines that will be running fifty years from now. They're going to keep building diesel engines for the next couple decades at least, even if the overall output decreases. They also service engines and intend to keep doing so. That means they're going to need people who can build and maintain those engines and all their parts for many years to come. But who wants to be trained in a dying technology? No one wants to pin their career on the horse and buggy when everyone is switching to Ford Model Ts.

So Cummins has two gaps to fill. They need people who under-stand hydrogen engines for the future, and they need people who understand diesel as it gets phased out. But the nature of these gaps is very different. With hydrogen, the company needs to train new people. With diesel, they need to hold on to some fraction of their current workforce and convince them to stick with the technology they already know—even though it's past its prime.

This is not a unique dilemma. If you know anything about how information is stored at banks and life insurance companies, you probably know that they still use the old COBOL programming in some capacity. That requires a certain number of programmers who understand COBOL to continue working, even though the world moved far beyond the COBOL coding language decades ago.

I've seen this kind of gap in my own backyard. I live in Fairfax County, where there used to be a public safety building that housed the fire and police departments. For years, the local government was planning to move to a new building because the old one had so many asbestos problems. In those circumstances, no one wanted to invest in the new HVAC system the building desperately needed just so it could be thrown away in a year or two. But that meant they had to keep servicing a system installed in the 1960s—a system that no one had made parts for in decades—until they constructed the new building and completed the move.

Every time the system needed a repair, the county had to fly up the one guy who still knew how to make the parts. He was retired in Florida, and the only way to keep the building open was to fill the gap with this one person's expertise.

Whether it's a huge company moving in a new direction or a local government building, the issue is the same. To pursue any strategy, you have to fill those gaps.

Two Types of Gap

The basics of gap are about as simple as math gets. You take the demand, subtract your supply, and see what's left. But as in basic arithmetic, this can lead to two different kinds of results: a surplus and a deficit.

Cummins has both in its transition to hydrogen. It has a current surplus of talent manufacturing its diesel engines, but a deficit in the hydrogen department. It also has a potential future deficit in diesel once the transition occurs.

Before we can pinpoint and fill the gaps in your organization, we need to take a moment to understand why the results of the equation come out the way they do.

Surplus

Finding a surplus in your supply might seem like a rarity—and in business as usual it can be. But it does still come up regularly. Most often, you'll see this when macroeconomic situations intervene. Recessions can create major surpluses in talent. As business slows down, companies will have a surplus in sales and production. Cutting those surplus jobs can create a surplus in HR and perhaps finance.

This also occurs in mergers and acquisitions. When Procter & Gamble bought Gillette, they had two departments for every function. They had two research and development departments, two finance departments, and so on. As P&G absorbed Gillette, they'd only need one of each. While the new company would likely have more people overall than either one did before, that would still leave surpluses in most areas.

The final way that companies most often arrive at a surplus is through technology. The great American miracle of the mid-twentieth century to the early twenty-first century saw productivity double in this country every few years. That incredible leap has slowed down tremendously, but technology will still continue to create surpluses in certain departments.

Advances in automation, for instance, mean utility companies will soon no longer need people to climb up pylons and trim trees. They'll have a surplus in that area. AI may create surpluses in HR, sales, or marketing in years to come.

Deficit

More than likely, when you are looking for gaps in your organization, you're thinking about deficits. Deficits often suggest the kind of environment business leaders are looking for. They show up in booming economies, in opportunities in emerging markets, and in major growth opportunities. They're often present when you introduce new products. In other words, deficits often suggest your company is growing and driving in new, exciting directions.

But this is not the only kind of deficit, and some forms are less positive. Deficits occur when an aging workforce retires. We've already discussed how the coming period when the boomers retire followed shortly after by Gen X will create deficits in leadership positions across most companies.

Deficits also develop from those changes in technology. Where those utility companies may soon have a surplus of workers to cut trees, they'll also have a deficit in workers who can operate and troubleshoot the technology. Those new positions may require a STEM degree, making the deficit gap harder to fill. And this is by no means a rare transition. Technology often creates surplus on the physical labor side while creating deficits in more advanced skills.

Another less obvious deficit can occur around location. Australian mining companies often have to get very creative with their labor deficits. The mines tend to be far away from population centers, and since they can't be moved, the mining companies have to offer a combination of incentives and creative scheduling to keep them operating. This same deficit plagues companies like Amazon who prefer to build their warehouses thirty or so miles outside every city. That gives them lower costs and cheaper labor while allowing them to provide same-day delivery to most customers. However, where that strategy works very well with fulfillment centers in New Jersey that serve New York City, massive deficits can occur in less densely populated areas. It's likely more difficult to staff the warehouse outside a city like Lincoln, Nebraska.

Finally, you find deficits in periods of high turnover. If morale is low or the company can't remain competitive in wages and benefits, deficits can start opening up across departments.

Moving into Fulfillment

As with Cummins, you may find that you have a mix of deficits and surpluses across your organization. Some departments may have a surplus of talent as you integrate new technology. Others may have deficits due to a combination of retirement, high growth opportunities, and the location of your office. Crucially, though, once you have clarity on the nature of these gaps, you can begin considering your fulfillment options.

Importantly, fulfillment is not a yes/no question. Instead, it's a matter of constraints and weights. Weights refer to your priorities. What do you care about most? What do you care about next most?

Weighing your priorities is important because every fulfillment effort will run into constraints that you can't work around. For instance, you are always going to have a financial constraint. Your gap may be twenty-five software developers with skills in a certain programming language. To bring in twenty-five new people with those skills might cost the company $8 million. But your finance may constrain you to spending $6 million.

You may also have location constraints. If your business is based in a city with a limited supply of the skill you need to fill, it may not be possible or economical to move operations where there is more supply. For instance, Intel has put billions into their chip factory in Taiwan. Even if there were better labor options elsewhere, they can't easily shift locations.

Alternatively, there may be constraints that come with filling a gap from another location. We've already discussed how outsourcing to other countries isn't as straightforward a win as many corporate leaders would like to imagine. There may be a huge amount of tech talent in India that you could hire for cheaper than in America, but that doesn't mean it's the easy and best solution every time.

In certain industries and for certain positions, you may also run up against regulatory constraints. You may only want four people in a position, but that doesn't matter if the government mandates that you have five. You may only need eight skills for a job, but regulations may require you to hire someone with two more.

Some companies end up constrained by previous deals. MetLife, as we've already seen, negotiated a great deal to bring part of their team to Charlotte. But now, any time they need to hire new talent to fill a gap, they have to find a way to get them to Charlotte.

I was with Microsoft when they were facing an antitrust lawsuit from the United States back in 2001. Canada offered to pay to move Microsoft across the border from Seattle to Vancouver. They sweetened the deal with a promise not to tax the company for ten years. In the end, that situation resolved itself, but if Microsoft had taken it, they would have faced new constraints with a smaller talent pool in Canada than the United States, as well as constraints around the number of work visas they could acquire each year.

Time can be a constraint as well. You need so many people, but you only have so long to fill the positions. The biggest delay in filling a gap is often not the background check or the two weeks' notice for someone to transition to your company—it's finding and interviewing the talent. On average, it takes forty-seven days to fill a job in America. Obviously, some hiring processes take longer—like those in place for executives and scientists. Others, like hiring line workers, go more quickly. But when you need people quickly, this can also constrain your fulfillment options.

Finally, there are external labor market constraints that can limit your fulfillment ambitions. This includes recessions and changes in geopolitics that make it difficult or impossible to hire talent in certain countries. In recent years, we've seen this play out in states that passed controversial laws that left some companies unwilling to shift resources to those states. The recent legal issues between Disney and the state of Florida are a famous example, as well as the infamous "bathroom bill" in North Carolina. In both cases, companies constrained themselves because of external political factors.

Facing all these constraints, you have to weigh priorities so you can focus on the gaps that matter most. Weighting will be different company to company and even department to department or division to division within an organization. A priority gap or priority fulfillment solution for HR may be different from the priority at R&D. It's leadership's job to balance these weights and get a little creative in how to fill gaps most effectively considering their constraints.

Fulfillment Options

You probably know the basics of your fulfillment options. You have the talent inside your company already. You can hire more direct labor by opening new full-time and part-time positions. There are contingent labor options through temp agencies and gig labor options through 1099 contracts that you might hire for specific tasks. Finally, you have the bots: AI, automation, and so on.

Each of these solutions offers different benefits and different costs. To make the best decision, you need your workforce planning model to offer you clarity on what those really look like. You can't always go with your default assumptions on this. For instance, we've just lived through a period in which the gig worker seemed to be the solution for everything. Put them on a contract, get the work done, and you don't have to pay benefits.

Gig workers are great when you have temporary work that might require a freelance expert in a certain skill. I've already mentioned the benefits of getting the same people to come in every year to close your books over a quarter. This can be much cheaper than keeping the same number of accountants on staff for the year. And if you have to scale down, you can cut gig workers more easily than staff. As a final benefit, by outsourcing such tasks, you no longer have to think about it. You can focus on what is core to your business.

So what's not to love? Well, there are constraints you have to deal with. You may run into issues around protecting your intellectual property. If that accountant was on staff, they could be trained to learn all the specific nuances of your company and your systems. You can't tell a gig worker how to do their job. You can't make them do it your way. You hire them to complete a task within a certain amount of time, and you have to let them complete it. That means you lose certain efficiencies. You lose the nuance that direct labor might provide.

You also lose the opportunity to distribute that talent. If you have brought that accountant in as a W-2 employee, you can review their skills like everyone else on your team. You may find that while you only need them for three months a year to work on the books, you need them for nine months in other departments. Without realizing it, you may have a second gap you've left unattended because you went with the easy and obvious fulfillment option.

One of the biggest considerations for the method of fulfillment you choose depends on how vital that role is to your operations. In every organization, there are choke points. If the work isn't done right in those positions, it can't forward. When you consider critical jobs, most people would point to a high-level leadership role like CEO, but you don't need a CEO for the company to run day to day. Instead, focus on those roles that would shut things down if they were left understaffed.

For instance, Georgia-Pacific makes paper products. To do that, they need someone to run the boiler at each of their plants. If that person is out for an extended period, the entire operation shuts down. They had a plant in Texas with only one full-time boiler operator. When he went out on disability, they could only run the plant part-time because the only other person who could work the boiler had limited availability.

The company did have an extra operator in Kansas City, but there were regulatory constraints. Namely, he wasn't licensed in Texas.

That's not the kind of position you want to trust to a gig worker. It's not something you want to have to fill temporarily. Instead, you want to fill that gap with the type of labor that offers the most resiliency. Otherwise, it can cost you far more than the wages and benefits of a single extra full-time employee.

This is not the only thing that might influence your fulfillment choices. As we've already discussed, some companies are constrained on location. They can't move operations easily. But with most white-collar work, it can be cheaper to simply open a new office where the supply is.

Talent clusters in certain locations, and your workforce planning model can show you where to find the right cluster for the particular talent you need. For instance, Coca-Cola moved its HR department down to a town outside of Tampa Bay because that was a large call center area. There was a ton of HR talent pooled in a relatively afford-able area. Opening the new office was far more efficient than trying to fill their deficits in an area with a limited supply.

Filling Gaps Can Create Gaps

In every fulfillment situation, companies are facing multiple factors. That's why, while the gap equation is basic arithmetic, fulfillment is actually multivariable calculus. Whenever considering fulfillment options, you have to consider time, quality, customer experience, growth strategies, regulations, productivity, intellectual property, risk, etc.—all of which are constraints. With so many variables, you have to be conscious of the fact that filling a gap might create another one elsewhere.

Sometimes, filling a gap creates a new vulnerability elsewhere. You can fill a gap that improves the quality of a product but reduces the speed of delivery, for instance. And filling a gap in one area can create new issues elsewhere in your organization.

In any company, there are very real budget constraints driven by the costs associated with production and what a product can be sold for. One cannot spend unlimited monies, only what you take in minus a reasonable profit for shareholders.

So if you have the objective of increasing your R&D outputs you can move resources from production, quality control, or elsewhere to R&D because they have the skill sets you need. This, as your workforce plan would indicate, allows you to increase your pipeline and, based on basic statistics, can be monetized to increase the number of new products that will successfully emerge and the profits the company will make off them.

But depending on the industry, that could be up to ten years down the road based on clinical studies, manufacturing changes, regulatory approvals, etc. In the near term, assuming resources are finite, moving those resources may slow down how much of the existing products can be produced or may cause production shifts between plants, resulting in greater costs of production. These trade-offs must be factored into the models. You will create gaps. That is not necessarily a bad thing; you just want it to be intentional and data driven.

We've just lived through a huge lesson in this "gap creep" during the pandemic. Up until COVID, just-in-time delivery was all the rage. Yet there was an obvious liability to this strategy. If you optimized your supply chain to be just in time at the factory, if one component was late to arrive, it could create cascading delays. It was just like the boiler operator going on disability for Georgia-Pacific. Nothing could work. Leadership responded to these issues by ordering larger quantities of materials. But that created more backlog for those manufacturers. Attempting to ease certain supply chains could lead to others backing up. It also created inflationary pressures and gaps in available supply. The problems became macro to the economy and not just micro to the specific company.

I'm sure we all remember the empty car lots and empty shelves where gaps in production were simply insurmountable for a time.

To limit "gap creep," you have to work your equation backward to label every area that gap touches. Sticking with just-in-time delivery, companies practicing this process have to start at the end point and chart all the contingencies that process affects. So if I want my product on a Target shelf when a customer reaches for it on Tuesday, the truck with that product has to leave the warehouse on Monday. That means the product has to be manufactured the Friday before and placed in its plastic container. And so on and so forth back to the very beginning of the process. Laying out the process shows all the links in the chain that are exposed to potential gaps when you make changes or face disruption.

The same is true for your workforce. There is no piece of a company that functions entirely independently. At times, the lines may be indirect, but they are present. Each process touches many others in a large organization. HR processes directly or indirectly touch on financial processes, and vice versa. The same is true across operations. If you fill a gap in HR, does that affect the financial constraints in R&D or SC&O? How will those limits affect your output going forward?

Understanding those links can help you prepare for potential gaps that may open when a priority gap is filled. When you put your processes to paper, you can visualize the "choke" points and the constraints and make more strategic decisions around those points.

Maybe it's OK if a back-office process runs more slowly and the emphasis is on production. But if that process is finance and you are required to report 10Q and 10K in a timely manner, then not only can you run afoul of regulators but you can also cause harm to your shareholders. In other words, this is, to be certain, a balancing act.

And ideally this doesn't become an either–or situation. When gaps are identified, mitigation strategies can be created. These are usually at the line manager level instead of the enterprise level. But the decisions made in your talent strategy should automatically identify those gaps and bring them to the attention of impacted parties so that they can create (within whatever business or workforce constraints that have been identified) a risk mitigation approach. In doing so, workforce planning improves the overall efficiency of how organizations run, and that monetizes quickly as work is done by qualified people when it needs to be done.

Comparing Your Gaps to Those of Competitors

You've already set benchmarks in your demand, but it's time to return to them here. Compare your benchmarks to external benchmarks set across your industry or across industries based on a functional capability. If you have one person in HR for 95 employees but competitors benchmark at 235 employees, you should ask questions. As we've seen, you may have good answers to those questions—as Microsoft did in the early 2000s—but the questions should still be considered. The aim here is to ensure decisions are made by design, not by default.

Those same benchmarks should be in place for other aspects of the job, such as compensation. What is the going rate for a project manager or a financial analyst across your industry? As we'll see in the next chapter, compensation is not everything when it comes to attracting and retaining talent, but you don't want to be overpaying or underpaying all the same—if for no other reason than it makes fulfillment more difficult. Overpaying increases your financial constraints, while underpaying makes it harder to fill a gap and to keep it filled.

The data on these benchmarks is easily available. Many organizations sell benchmarking studies. Academic institutions, consulting companies, and specialty providers such as TalentNeuron, Mercer, and Aon all offer industry-specific surveys. PricewaterhouseCoopers also offers them through their Saratoga Institute. Some software vendors, Visier for example, collect data in the aggregate from their customers and sell this as normalized benchmarks. These are just examples and not recommendations, but they point to a wide variety of sources available to companies of all shapes and sizes.

Expanding your understanding of the nature of your gaps and how best to fill them compared to your competitors opens up new insights. In particular, you can start to discover whether your network engineers look different from everyone else's. If they do, what can you do to change that? Do you hire more? Do you train differently? Are you losing your best talent? If so, what can you do about that?

In other words, simply following this process leads us naturally from workforce planning into the world of talent management.

CHAPTER 7

Talent Management

The US Navy may or may not be right about the threats that America will face in the future, but they definitely know how to plan for the workforce they'll need to face the threats they predict. They know how many pilots they'll need to meet every potential opponent they've gamed out. They know how many of the pilots that they currently have will leave in the next few years to go fly for United Airlines and Delta. They know how many will stay in their current positions and how many they'll promote. They know how many they need to recruit to fill these gaps. They even know how many will wash out in the training programs.

They have a sense of how many pilots will be replaced by the technology that's coming online today. As more missions are unmanned, they know the skills necessary to pilot drones compared to the skills for piloting a Super Hornet. They have a sense of the mix of recruits they need in order to put the right people with the right skills in the right positions.

But these are all just numbers on a screen. To actually act on these numbers takes something more. The Navy has to figure out how to recruit these new pilots. They have to know who, exactly, to promote, what training they should actually offer, and to whom. They need to build units that have not just the right set of skills but the right personalities. They need to station the right people at the right bases.

And that takes something more than workforce planning. It requires talent management.

Managing Your New Plan

Talent management serves the same function in the military that it does in business. Workforce planning is about getting numbers that prophesy your needs for your preferred strategy. Talent management is about the execution on those numbers.

Once you have your workforce planning model up and running, your numbers will look something like what we've already described in the book. It will generate a set of graphs for your HR department, and these graphs will tell them about all the various parts of your workforce plan. It will show where you have a surplus of five people and where you have a deficit of thirty. It'll show when you need to fill each gap and from which sources. It will tell them what training you need to offer, and so on across all your recruiting, training, and other HR functions.

For instance, your workforce planning model may prophesy your strategy requires fifty-six new system engineers, twenty-five new financial analysts, and thirty-four new HR generalists. It'll lay out how many people you need to hire in each of these positions in each of the upcoming quarters. It will also tell your HR team where your turnover is going to be most likely. It may predict that you'll lose 8 percent of your current employees over the next year and where those losses are most likely to be heaviest and lightest.

Crucially, your model should also be able to cast an eye toward the future. It should be able to tell your team where the company has a skill gap and when new gaps will become prevalent. This is invaluable because many of the most significant gaps your company will face with new technology don't show up on day one; they show up three years later. This will give you the head start you need to recruit and develop training for that future gap.

This is all extremely valuable information, but it isn't the end of the process because now you have some execution questions you have to answer. How fast are you going to move on your workforce plan? What strategies will you use to attract talent to your organization? How are you going to assess employees and what rewards will you tie to those assessments? Do you buy the training, or do you build it yourself? How are you going to incentivize employees to stick around? How fast should you promote people on average? At what levels? What should your organizational structure look like? Should it be a pyramid? A diamond? Should it be flat?

This is all talent management. Talent management is where you apply your company culture to your workforce plan. It's where you make the key decisions about how you're going to implement strategies that respond to the numbers you see on those graphs.

In other words, having the data in front of you is a great start, but now it's time to manage your talent in the way that best fits your company.

The importance of this step might be most easily seen in an extreme example. Let's imagine Company A has two workforce planning models that it runs to consider the various ways it can fill some critical deficits in its talent. One model lays out how Company A can hire, contract, and train to fill those gaps. The other model offers a path to fulfillment through merging with a competitor, Company B.

Talent management immediately comes into play with a huge, critical decision. Neither model will tell Company A's leadership which strategy to choose. Leadership will have to set priorities around overall strategy and company culture.

Let's say Company A decides to go with the merger. This decision leads to all kinds of new talent management concerns. For instance, someone has to identify the priority talent the company wants to hold on to as the two businesses merge. The workforce plan can tell HR that Company A had two hundred people in one position, Company B had another two hundred people, and the new company will only need three hundred people total in that area. But talent management is necessary to identify the right people to hold on to. Who are the three hundred Company A wants to keep, and who are the one hundred they should let go?

This is only the start of Company A's talent management considerations. There are also decisions to be made on org design. How flat should the new company be? Should it keep Company A's structure or Company B's structure? Or should a new structure be put in place?

Talent management is also in decisions about merging cultures between the companies. This is a hairier process than it might seem at first. Most would assume that the larger company's culture should remain intact while the smaller company adjusts to it. But that isn't always the right decision. Settling on the right mix of the two companies' cultures is usually the best practice, but once again, it requires talent management to make that call.

Employee Life Cycle Wheel

M&A is an extreme example of talent management. It usually doesn't play such a large and noticeable role in day-to-day operations. But it does still touch on every aspect of the employee life cycle. This is the path that every employee follows within an organization. Every employee goes through these same stages—source, integrate, optimize, and connect. Essentially, the life cycle takes us through finding talent, hiring talent, training talent, deploying talent, and transitioning talent out of the company.

TALENT LIFE CYCLE

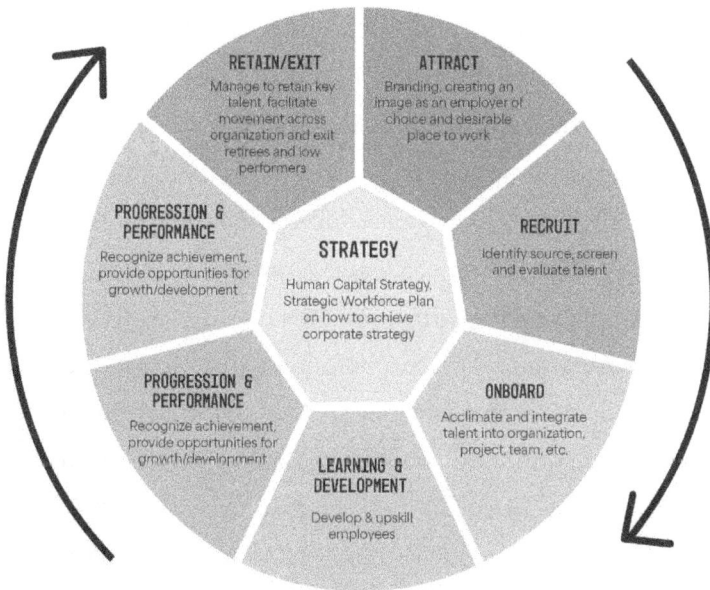

The nature of these steps may look different for different positions. How you source a cashier is very different from how you source a new head of sales, for instance. And succession for a CEO is nothing like succession for a network administrator.

Still the cycle is the same. And every company circles through it constantly. As some employees cycle out of your business, you need to attract new ones. As you develop some employees, others are being deployed for the first time. And so on.

Most of your regular uses of talent management fall within the scope of this wheel. Workforce planning gives you the numbers to fill in throughout this wheel, but how you implement those numbers takes talent management.

Recruitment

No matter how low your turnover, you will always have to hire people from the outside at some point. That's why sourcing, or recruitment, begins the employee life cycle. Once again, your workforce planning model can help immensely in this process. Where previously you most likely followed the same process as about 90 percent of companies out there, taking the budget for the fiscal year, authorizing for so many new hires across various divisions, and leaving the rest to HR, you'll now have far greater clarity. You'll know how many people you need in each job family in each quarter and all the skills they need to possess.

Just as importantly, a great workforce planning model can tell you where to look for that talent. Instead of trying to blanket a region, a state, or even a city, you can narrow your target down to the area where most of the talent you need resides. For instance, LA Metro is responsible for the light rail and buses across America's second-largest city. They often have a deficit in bus drivers. Each driver has to possess a commercial driver's license. LA Metro's response to those deficits has traditionally been to run city-wide ads and go out to local high schools. They hold events and try to attract interested parties across the entire LA community.

But with better workforce planning data, they could target their resources to the areas of the city in which people already have commercial driver's licenses and avoid those areas where they are unlikely to find interest. Instead of wasting money on billboards in Long Beach, they could focus on the larger pool of talent in the City of Industry.

Again, this is all possible through your workforce planning model, but you still have to execute on it. In the first place, you have to have a process for opening those positions in your hiring system. You have to decide where the person's actually going to sit in your organization and the name of their position. This can be done manually, or it can be automated. There's no right answer. It's what's going to work for what you're trying to do. How are people going to sign off on opening these positions? Is there an email chain? Is it someone pushing a button? Does the system automatically approve so long as it's part of the workforce plan?

Talent management requires you to work through these mechanics.

Once that's done, you have to decide on your sourcing strategy for these openings. Even with refined data on the location of a pool of talent, you have to decide how you will reach it. Are you running internet ads? Are you using Indeed? Are you using headhunters? Are you visiting college campuses? Are you cold calling other companies?

Once you have some candidates, how are you going to assess skills and find the right fit? Are you going to do behavioral interviews? Are you going to do case-based interviews? Are you going to do panel interviews? Are you going to give them personality tests of some kind?

And how long are you going to spend on this for each position? The timeline to hire an executive may be ten months. Multiple assembly-line workers can be hired in a week. What is the timetable for each position you're filling?

And who is going to run it? The people sourcing your executive team should be different from those hiring at other levels.

I recently spoke to a senior vice president whose sole responsibility was recruiting for the company's executive team. He'd been promoted from handling experience recruiting—filling positions for those who have ten to fifteen years of experience. The process he was running went from taking two to three weeks to an entire year.

The workforce plan could tell him what position he needed to fill. It could tell him where to look for the best candidates. But the company still needed a process. It still had to manage the sourcing of that talent.

Onboarding

Onboarding mostly falls within the scope of talent management. What does a new employee need to know about their position within your company and about your company culture to be a success? What processes do they need to be familiar with? What does the company need to know about the new employee? What training do they require at the outset? What team would they best slot into?

At the same time, talent management accounts for the time it will take to fully onboard those new recruits. It may take six months before a new employee is fully integrated and hitting their production numbers. What are you going to do in the meantime to avoid a lag in production? To account for this, you may have to ramp up the number of contractors you use temporarily as you bring the new recruits up to speed.

Training

In the future, workforce planning will probably take the step to assign individual employees to specific training, but for now, that's still a management process. HR can plan for training, finance can budget for it, but the line managers still need to assign individuals to training.

And that's just part of talent management's role in developing your talent. Let's say you have ten people with level-four agile skills when you need thirty-five. If you have enough people with adjacent skills, you can train the twenty-five people up to that level. But how do you do that? Who gets the training? And do you do it in the classroom? Do you do it in casework? Do you do it with books? Do you outsource it?

This is where culture often plays a role. Given your workforce and your company's culture, what works best for you?

For instance, Duke Energy has a "training by doing" policy with its line repair people. While someday these workers are likely to be replaced entirely through automation, for now, their work is still extremely important and extremely dangerous. To reduce the risk, Duke gives each worker a VR headset. When a worker pulls up to the power lines or the transformer they're repairing, they scan a QR code that brings up the exact model they'll be working on. They then put on the VR headset and do the work virtually while sitting in their car. That allows them to instantly train and prep for the work before doing anything in real life.

This takes more time, but it also vastly reduces risk. That saves lives. It lowers insurance premiums. It keeps workers active in the field. It's a huge win—one the workforce planning model had nothing to do with. That was the product of expert talent management.

Measurement and Promotion

We've already discussed the importance of implementing assessment within your organization. Thanks to your workforce planning model, you'll know the skills you need to see represented in each position.

You'll also have more data on who possesses those skills—whether they show up in the current job or not.

But you still have to assess your people and track the development of their skills. That requires decisions on how you will measure those skills. You'll need the tools to measure your core, technical, and leadership skills and metrics that show where each employee scores.

By managing your skill measurement, you can make better decisions on promotion—another area of talent management largely left untouched by workforce planning models. And once you decide who to promote, you have several additional talent management tasks to consider. What kind of training are you going to offer ahead of that promotion? How many direct reports will you place under a newly promoted manager? One is too few. Six would be unwieldy for someone new to a management position. Perhaps you start with two or three, but what is the mechanism through which that new manager increases the number of their direct reports until they have a full team?

The only way to determine this is through management.

Engagement and Retention

Every company has turnover. And every company wants some turnover. You need to refresh your workforce, bring in new ideas, and transition out your weakest team members while bringing in better talent. But there's an ideal number you want to hit—one that's specific to your industry and your business.

Your workforce planning model will help with this. It might tell you that you have 23 percent turnover and that you want to aim for 16 percent instead. Going lower, say to 8 percent, might be even better, but your model will show if the cost is simply too high to achieve that. So 16 percent it is. But how do you do that?

Some of the work here can be done through the most obvious changes. You could offer everyone a raise, for instance. Or you could start giving out spot bonuses. But while money is the first recourse for managers who want to retain their talent, it is often the least effective lever you have.

Part of the reason money is such a popular talent management tool is because it's the easiest lever to pull. "I'm going to give you a 3 percent raise, please don't quit" is the most obvious retention tactic imaginable. And who turns down more money? People are always grateful for a raise or a bonus.

The problem, though, is that after a few months, those same grateful employees adjust to the increase in their pay. And if you haven't changed anything else, they're still just as likely to leave. You also put yourself into a bidding war with your competition. If the only reason someone is staying is because you pay them better than your rivals, your rivals could always up their bid.

That's not to say money is inconsequential. If you severely underpay talent, they will leave. But when you're already paying at the level of the competition, it can have a limited impact on retention. Think back to chapter 2's story about Cencora. At some point, they topped out at a wage they could pay that would reduce turnover. The difference between $22 an hour and $24 an hour was negligible for them.

If you want to improve your retention numbers, you have to look elsewhere. And the thing most people are looking for is better talent management. They want to work in a place where they feel they are being fully utilized. They want to feel like they are a part of something. People like being on the leading edge. They like feeling they're at the top of their profession. They want to be surrounded by people with great talent just like themselves. They want a good team environment.

They want good benefits. They want bosses who are responsive to them. All of this falls under the scope of talent management.

Some of this can be provided through training. Some can be done through opportunities to grow within the company and do other jobs. Cultural changes, access to newer technologies, more interesting projects, more flexibility in work hours, more flexibility in how employees do their work: these changes are far more likely to drive down your turnover numbers.

And you can drive them down further simply by improving your management talent and strategies. Top talent want managers who actually listen to them. They want the ability to change how the company does things. Those are the changes that give people a real reason to stick around.

Many of these adjustments can be done in a relatively straightforward manner using tools you already have at hand. You can assemble better teams using the personality tests you've already run for demand and supply. Reviewing your turnover numbers may show you if certain managers are having a particularly negative effect on their teams. If the company has an 8 percent turnover rate and one manager is seeing 24 percent, that should be investigated. You can also review your benefits and solicit input from your workers.

All of these changes create an environment people don't want to leave. And all of them are built around talent management decisions you'll have to make within your organization.

Leave Room for Your Gut

Workforce planning and talent management are 80 percent science, 20 percent gut. While your workforce planning model will give you a lot of clarity on what needs to be done and where, you're still going to have to make judgment calls, set priorities, and create the systems through which you can deliver on the plan.

At the end of the day, there are still going to be decisions to make, strategies to implement, and processes to review and adjust.

I recently went through a round of interviews for an executive position. Now, at such a high level, you expect this process to take time. But this one took nine separate interviews. Did the company really need to see me nine times before they could make a call? That's more effort than most businesses put into choosing their CEO.

In the end, they simply struggled to make the big call, and their process reflected that. That's still going to be leadership's role. Whether it's putting your company's cultural stamp on recruitment, changing a certain process to reduce turnover, or adding a new assessment tool to track your talent's progress, no computer is going to tell you if that's the right or wrong policy. That's going to be your call.

But with better workforce planning models and talent management strategies, that call should now be easier to make.

PART III

INSTALLATION

CHAPTER 8

Building Stakeholder Support

The potential benefits of installing an elite workforce planning model and partnering it with improved talent management are immense. A major oil company I've worked with saw their retention rates increase by over 24 percent and the number of open positions decrease by almost 12 percent in their hardest-to-fill positions—Wildcatters and Petroleum Engineers—as they established new refineries.

Simply by harnessing the prophetic powers of workforce planning, leadership aligned their talent in a way that better fit with employee ambitions and needs while allowing the company to move resources around the globe to staff positions. It's hard to overstate how much that could change the company's future prospects. Proper staffing can reduce the amount of time it takes to get a refinery on line by as much as eighteen to twenty-four months, allowing a multibillion dollar investment to get from ROI to profitability in five years instead of almost ten. Additionally, these refineries serve as the training grounds for the company's blue- and white-collar future leaders.

And keep in mind, those benefits aren't the only value here. When they are able to get to profitability sooner, it not only increases shareholder value but allows them to deliver product to local markets at lower cost, benefiting consumers and business customers alike—thanks to workforce planning.

Of course, to realize these results, leadership had to agree to do the hard work of installing this system in the first place. The process of reaching that consensus looks different at different companies. In this company's case, operations and finance led the way, and HR, as well as several other parts of the company, were very reluctant participants. It was only once they started seeing the results that everyone became believers. Ultimately, HR became evangelical about extending the model to the other parts of the business. In fact, when the division presidents were informed of what was going on in the chemical division, there was immediate desire to just throw money at the challenges they were having and duplicate what they were seeing in the sister organization. It was a challenge to slow them down and ensure an orderly and well-thought-out implementation and rollout.

Getting every stakeholder on board is always difficult, but it's a process every company has to go through. To see the best results from workforce planning and talent management, you want to secure the buy-in of everyone who will play a role in the success of these systems. And securing buy-in requires some thoughtful strategy.

The Three-Legged Stool

Strategic workforce planning and talent management reside on a three-legged stool for their support. Those legs each represent a key function at least partly responsible for greenlighting the model, building the model, maintaining the model, and enjoying the benefits of the model.

One leg is finance. Because workforce planning requires funding and will also result in savings, finance has an obvious role to play here.

The second leg is human resources. This division will be responsible for the talent management side of workforce planning. It will be acting on the prophesies that come out of the model. They are the executers, and it is in the execution the value is realized. The third leg is operations. As a money-making function within the business, this division pulls the most weight of the three. Its chief concern is to see services fulfilled efficiently and affordably. Workforce planning and talent management can help on both fronts.

Additionally, in industries such as manufacturing that have a quality assurance function, they can also become a key stakeholder and a fourth leg of the stool, as they often help drive staffing levels and measure staff effectiveness. We won't focus on their role here, but suffice to say, the strategies related below can help this function buy into workforce planning as well.

Whichever leg you represent in your company, you have to earn the support of the other two (or three). If you run finance, you need operations and HR on board. Likewise, if you're HR, you need finance and operations. Operations can technically insist that HR and finance implement these systems since, again, it usually has more power within the organization, but it's still better to secure support than to force compliance. The same may be true for finance. Finance controls budgets, and with that comes power, but it still wants consensus to drive something like this forward. HR may also someday be in this power position since over the last decade it has gone from an order-taking support function to a true strategic and analytics-driven partner. But that transformation has not been smooth or completed in most organizations.

In other words, each function needs the support of the other two.

These discussions will always involve unique conversations based on individual relationships and company culture. Still, there are some general guidelines that can help win over support from your partners in this process.

Finance to the Other Legs

While not as powerful as operations, finance is still a power player in business. Nothing really happens unless finance signs off and says the company has the money. Accountants have become central to modern business strategy. Business leaders have gotten used to making decisions off of finance's dashboards. For decades, every manager has been able to pull up for their P/L on their financial dashboard and see the health of their organization.

For all these reasons, finance bringing workforce planning to the table will have a lot of influence even without much effort to convince the other legs of the stool.

However, you want both of those legs to hold up this system with their full strength and commitment. In an effort to win that support, you should start with operations. With operations and finance on the same page, HR will follow. That doesn't mean you should ignore their concerns (more on those in a moment), but you should still be able to see the models implemented.

When speaking to operations, focus your approach on the benefits from operations' perspective. With better numbers and longer forecasts, finance can promise to free up capital for operations to do other things. Finance will be able to tell operations exactly what the company is spending on labor and where savings can be found.

Instead of having to leave a little extra to cover unexpected costs or searching in the couch cushions because the company never knows quite what they are spending on labor, the whole company can move forward with far more accuracy.

Savings and efficiency should convince operations, but HR is a different matter. HR can feel threatened when the impetus for workforce planning models comes from finance (or operations, as we'll see). Often, when finance approaches HR about workforce planning, what the head of HR hears is that finance wants to lay off half of HR's staff.

For that reason, it's valuable to frontload your discussion with the importance of HR in this process. After all, HR is going to have the majority of the responsibility and workload when running talent management. That means there is no reason to assume huge cuts will be coming to HR.

At the same time, workforce planning offers HR the chance to fulfill its potential as a strategic advisor. This is often a long-term goal for the division. Traditionally, HR is an order taker. It's the corporate policemen and handles things like benefits. But HR has the potential to earn a seat at the table where the business determines its strategy.

When HR signs on to workforce planning, it can be a better strategic support, helping the business in new ways as it ensures the company has the right talent across all operations. This allows business leaders to make contingency plans instead of being blindsided by surprises in its labor supply. If leadership knows a quarter ahead of time that there will be a crucial gap, the company has time to pivot. HR can lead that process.

HR to the Other Legs

HR isn't always skeptical of workforce planning. There are many department leaders who fully embrace the value of these models. Their mission is to convince the more powerful legs of the stool to go along. How do you get finance to loosen the purse strings enough to build this model in the first place? How do you prove to operations this isn't a waste of time taking focus away from delivering to customers or more directly cutting costs?

In both cases, the argument should focus on the value of data-driven talent decisions. This is the language of finance and operations.

When HR approaches finance, the argument is fairly straightforward: "You already do this. You already forecast labor costs and budgets. I'd like us to do this together."

For the finance stakeholders, you can also focus on the cost savings that will come once the model is up and running. Additionally, the model will offer finance new benefits. They'll have more granularity in their numbers. Instead of a one-year forecast they update every six months, the workforce planning model should allow them to run things quarterly and project out multiple years—with those first two years being particularly accurate.

We've already looked at scenarios that show the value of this accuracy. For instance, instead of finance budgeting $100,000 to fill a certain number of positions over a whole year, they can budget $50,000 for the second half of year one and hold off on the other $50,000 until the second year. They can then use the other $50,000 elsewhere.

That same idea is extremely appealing to operations. But you can sweeten the deal further for that function by pointing out that operations will be able to commit to their business with far more confidence. The reason they can be so confident is because the workforce planning model can ensure that the right talent with the right skills is in the right positions across the organization to deliver on operations' promises.

Instead of fearing unexpected gaps or falling behind in skills, operations can be certain the company knows all its gaps and is addressing them well ahead of the point those gaps could lead to delays or additional expenses.

Operations to the Other Legs

If you are operations, you have the ability to simply set the course for this. You can absolutely ignore the concerns of finance and HR and simply command this system be put in place. But that isn't the best way to secure buy-in and support from those functions, and since most of the responsibility and value will come in those areas, you still want their real support.

It makes sense for operations to start from a place of strength, letting finance and HR know that you need this, and you need finance and HR to make it happen. But you have to be aware of the concerns such discussions may raise in those two departments. When operations pushes for workforce planning and new talent strategies, it often feels like the COO is telling the CFO and head of HR that their teams are failing.

After all, if leadership was effective in managing costs and talent, why would operations want this system in the first place? The COO must feel that finance and HR are letting the company down—or at least that's how it can sound. And if you come in commanding the change, it reinforces that sense.

Once again, since finance is the more powerful leg here, you should start by convincing them. And this argument is fairly simple. There are numerous potential cost savings and process improvements for finance in these models. It's possible to increase output, as that pharmaceutical company did, without increasing expenses. That's the case even if finance is currently well run.

With HR, you can reframe these values in language that speaks to that department's concerns. I often suggest operations call this "evidence-based HR" when explaining its value. That communicates how workforce planning will allow HR to make better decisions because they know exactly what they have to work with.

And then you can show HR how this allows them to better look out for the people in the company. With more data, they can support talent at a higher level. With the right people on the right teams doing the right work, everyone is happier, more engaged, and more productive. People feel they're getting paid what they're worth. The models can create clarity on career paths, helping train and promote the best people. And HR will be tasked with executing on all those priorities.

Don't Forget IT

Before moving on, it's important to single out one final stakeholder you shouldn't forget: your IT team. They will have to maintain the technology systems necessary to make this scalable and sustainable. They aren't a large enough stakeholder here to be a leg of your stool, but it's still always better to have them on board from the beginning.

For some companies, of course, the IT team tasked with maintaining your workforce planning models will be under HR already. This would make it easier to keep them up to date as the project develops.

If this isn't the case, though, it's still generally recommended you bring them to the table early. They may not be invited into the discussion, but having them present communicates their importance.

Unexpected Benefits to Convince Every Stakeholder

These suggestions are not exhaustive. As I said above, every department and department leader will be unique. And there may be other stakeholders you have to consider at your company. You may need to convince the CEO or speak to the board to get approval. There could be concerns from investors or a particular department that may be affected by changes suggested by workforce planning. Perhaps your company works with a labor union. They may require certain accommodations.

Each of these stakeholders will require the same kind of nuanced and focused conversation as the three legs of the stool. At this point, though, you should have plenty of ammunition to cover the value of these changes. However, to aid in those discussions, I recommend focusing on the two major benefits to workforce planning and talent management that highlight its value to almost all stakeholders.

Getting Every Person to the Right Position

I was recently talking to someone who works in HR for the government. She was lamenting the fact that she couldn't fill an important position. As I dug into the problem with her, it turned out that she actually had two good candidates. The problem was that the policy for her department was to interview at least three people before making an offer. While she waited for another application, she was afraid the two candidates would find other work.

Workforce planning can help eliminate these unnecessary choke points on your talent. It can help you find the right people, put them in the right positions, and accelerate their rise to the position that best suits their skills. However, most corporate policies are not written to fully leverage the analytic power available in the modern workplace. Some will need to be revisited and potentially changed. That does not mean the spirit and intent of the original policy will be lost, just that it is time to modernize.

This acceleration isn't limited to those you hope will reach the top of leadership. Most employees will never get to the C-Suite, but that doesn't mean your company should ignore their progress. You want them in the position where they can do their best work—and you want them there as soon as possible.

With workforce planning and talent management, you know the skills each person possesses. You know their personality type and temperament. You know the training and experience they need before they can move up the organization. And you can discover all this using a scientific, unbiased approach.

This allows you to turn the Peter Principle on its head. Instead of seeing everyone rise until above their highest level of competence, you can get them to that ceiling as soon as possible and keep them where they can do their best work.

Operational Benefits

The cost savings of the oil company I worked with are real, as they always are for organizations that implement these systems. There are huge savings that come from hiring more effectively. Huge savings from promoting and training better. You'll net real savings in labor because you won't have to overstaff anymore. You'll see savings by always having resiliency in every labor choke point in your organization. You'll save in seeing turnover hit an ideal point for your company.

Savings from improved effectiveness and efficiency, increased sales/customer satisfaction, or lowered costs improving profit margin are softer to measure. Many factors go into them, and talent is only one of them. Still, with over 90 percent of companies that invest in workforce planning seeing those benefits, it stands to reason that it is a major contributor to those realized improvements.

Across the board, you get savings operationally from doing things once the right way at the right time. The easiest example of this is recruitment. Let's say a good recruiter in your company can handle thirty to forty jobs at a time. That's a decent average for those recruiting knowledge workers. And if they're that good, they probably hire four to five people in a month. Over the course of a year, that equates to maybe 250 hires.

Basic workforce planning suggests that if you're going to hire 5,000 people, you need around twenty good recruiters. But if you know that you need 1,000 hires this quarter, 1,500 the next quarter, and the rest in the third quarter, that changes how you deploy your recruiters. You can target your resources more effectively, reducing your budget and achieving better results.

That may require fewer recruiters. It can save on labor costs. I can also help you achieve the ultimate results at the pace that is best for your strategy. You can eliminate inefficiencies, cut costs, and deliver more effectively.

Let me give you one final example. We have all experienced training in the workplace that we do not really absorb and apply. That can be because of how the training was designed or delivered, but more often than not, it is because after we complete the course, we do not go back and immediately apply what we have learned. Adult learners improve most when they can take "classroom" learning and apply it in the real world while the new knowledge is fresh in their heads.

Instead, what often happens is training is rolled out to support a corporate initiative, and in the rush to get everyone through the training, that journey is completed before the processes or changes are ready for employees to apply it. Months go by, and when the changes are finally brought on line, the employees only remember part of what they learned. That leads to either less efficient uptake and utilization or the need to retrain and again complete a course they have already completed. In either case, you are either not realizing the full benefits or delivering training twice at an additional cost.

In other words, improving the process of training and bringing changes on line can save everyone time and save the company money.

And everyone in the company wants that.

Preach Patience

The reason it's possible to convince every stakeholder of the value of workforce planning and talent management is that the benefits they offer are real. And those benefits are spread across the company. In total, when done at the enterprise level, these systems should save you between 18 and 23 percent on your labor costs. Those savings are possible because of the reduced head count, reduced salaries, and improved efficiency. These systems don't even require layoffs to see those savings. They can be realized simply by adjusting hiring, promotions, training, and organization.

But importantly, there is one word of warning here. While those benefits will come, they don't come immediately.

At one pharmaceutical company I worked with, there were significant savings that came with the additional drug testing they were performing each year. But it took five years to see the full benefits. It was three years before these efforts even broke even. That is because pharmaceuticals is in the R&D business, which means their profit cycles are very long.

Most businesses see the financial benefits much sooner—and efficiency benefits even sooner than that. But it still takes time to build the system and adjust it. When you talk to stakeholders, you want to be realistic about when they'll see the value of the investment.

So long as they know how long they have to wait, the benefits here are usually enough to convince everyone to get on board. At that point, you'll have the all-clear to implement these processes into your organization.

CHAPTER 9

Implementing the Process

Like Microsoft back in the early 2000s, Apple organizes its company as a decentralized creative environment. It's a federalized model of organization, in which people develop Apple products mostly in isolation from other teams. The people who develop the apps are almost completely independent of those who design the hardware for the iPhones. And the hardware people are similarly separated from those developing the next version of MacOS.

This is not new knowledge; it is a very effective way of running a creative company. There are countless business school case studies that you can easily locate that talk to both the models at Apple and the models at Microsoft and why those two companies have been so successful over decades. No doubt you'll also find the stories of what happens when those models are changed without sufficient fore-thought and analysis, including the stumbles these very companies have made (and notably recovered from).

This federalized system is enormous, as you might expect at one of the largest and most successful companies on the planet. It includes the large teams you'd think of like those designing the next iPhone.

But there are also smaller teams doing things like refining the GPS system running in the background of the iPhone and Apple Watch.

There are, of course, certain loose associations. They all build products that will interact on Apple's various products and use the same operating systems. But there is no common organizational system for talent. In fact, these teams don't even talk about talent the same way. They've developed multiple models to forecast talent demand and supply.

Implementing the workforce planning and talent management ideas we've covered in this book all at once at an organization that large would have been daunting—and working on the enterprise level would also have gone against Apple's corporate philosophy. So when Apple started looking to improve organization, they decided to start smaller. In this case, they decided to work with the team in the apps department that develops the internal application marketplace. This team designs the parameters that allow third-party apps to work with iOS.

The aim was to install these new systems in that one division to both prove out the model's capabilities and allow an intentional scale from that point. Essentially, once installed there, they could install it with minimal adjustments and minimal expense in any area leadership thought would benefit. If it would be useful in the Apple TV division, it could easily be implemented. If there was more to be gained with the teams that were building the next version of Pages or Numbers, it was just as easy to install there.

With this starting point in place, they set about explaining the implementation process to the app store project managers while also listening to their management pain points. In particular, they needed greater clarity on capacity and improved budgetary control. Too often, project managers were being asked to complete nine projects when they seemed to only have capacity to complete six. This is not a challenge unique to tech companies by any stretch of the imagination.

At the same time, it was extremely difficult to know when workers were maxed out on their workload. Apple's overall approach was a mix of waterfall, agile organization, and development models—which, again, were custom tailored by each department. This allowed the company to work carefully on certain projects and get others to market faster as necessary. However, it left management with significant blind spots. They couldn't see which of their DevOps people had capacity and which didn't.

With DevOps team members jumping from one three-week job to the next five-week assignment, project managers struggled to continually leverage each person's skill set.

The solution to both problems was a better understanding of skills, supply, and budget. Project managers needed visibility into each member's skill set and bandwidth. With greater clarity, they could see if two DevOps people within the scrum had the right skills and enough capacity to step into a project at a crucial moment. Along with creating that visibility, they needed added clarity on budget constraints and project requirements. That would allow management to see whether there was money in the budget to bring in a contractor for specialized work when an entire team had maxed out its capacity.

In that apps department, just building the ability to see what the different projects were, the available budget, the skills of the various team members, and how people were deployed allowed project managers to complete, on average, eight of the nine projects they were tasked with. That was a 33 percent improvement on production without it changing Apple's budget.

That was more than enough proof for Apple. They kept those gains and started looking for where to expand these systems next.

The Piece-by-Piece Approach

Apple's piece-by-piece approach is very common. While building workforce planning models and talent management strategies at the enterprise level can net 18–24 percent savings, as I mentioned in the last chapter, often, it makes more sense for companies to start smaller and scale. Once the system is in place, it usually is easy and cheap to expand.

Once you have committed to implementing the ideas we've covered in this book, the most important thing to recognize is that there is no one way to install these systems. While most companies start small, starting small can look very different from business to business. In chapter 5, I told the story of a large telecom company. They installed the system across the entire organization, but they only used the supply step.

This is only one part of the process, but this model of piece-by-piece installation can still net massive results. If you follow that telecom company's lead and simply implement, you will have a better view of your workforce. This visibility can drive reductions in hiring and reduce turnover. These improvements can raise morale across your workforce, which can drive higher productivity and further reduce turnover. Conservatively, companies often see 1–3 percent labor savings here.

Many companies, though, do not start with supply but with demand forecasting. If you just do demand forecasting and nothing else, you can run your budgeting operations off that forecast. That more accurate forecasting can save you 4–8 percent on your labor. It can improve your financial rigor, which impacts capital spending.

With either demand or supply, you can get a better sense of your gaps and your fulfillment options. With a stronger grasp of fulfillment, you won't need as many recruiters. You can make sure you're training the right people with the right skills—and you're training only once. That can lead to 5–15 percent in savings, depending on how inefficient your HR department is. This is reflected in the 2023 Gartner Market Guide for Workforce Management.

These percentages hold true even if you scale down. You can start with a single step in a single department, or even a single division, and see savings. You can simply make sales run more efficiently with a better sense of your supply of skills, for instance. The savings will still be there.

In fact, if you do nothing else but formalize and standardize how you convert business demand to workforce demand and forecast that alone, you will still see cost savings and improvements.

And those savings can help pay for the rest of the process.

The important thing to remember here is that these are bottom-up, not top-down systems. And when you install them from bottom-up, you can start anywhere, at any size, and with any steps.

Go Slow to Go Fast

Once you determine where you are going to start, it's time to get everyone on board and make sure everyone understands their role in implementing the model and improving talent management.

This is how it was done at Apple. They put the forty project managers responsible for the app department in a room to teach them how to install it and run it for their teams. Many were not thrilled by the idea—and for very understandable reasons. Remember, each one of these managers had been instructed to run their teams however they felt worked best. There were fifteen different methodologies in that room. Suddenly, we were asking them to put in extra work in order to standardize a single process—a completely foreign idea at Apple.

It's possible here to dictate the change, but it's always better to use a combination of carrots and sticks to get everyone rowing in the same direction. One of the reasons you want everyone to actually buy in is that you need them to keep updating their data. As the technology goes online, such updates will become automatic and won't require an extra management layer, but until then, it takes individual effort. That means managers have to dedicate extra time before they can see the real value in these systems.

This is a classic "go slow to go fast" situation. Eventually, the results will make work more efficient and require less effort, but the slow period up front can be extremely frustrating.

This was certainly the case at Apple. For about four weeks, each project manager had to spend an extra three or so hours on these updates—on top of all their usual responsibilities. But even in that period, there was a noticeable improvement in how their teams were operating. Tasks were getting completed more quickly. While their lives were getting worse, their teams' lives were getting better.

That was enough to maintain their support through that painful early stage. As soon as the models went online, the project managers got their hours back and got to enjoy the new visibility they'd been lacking.

Create a Fair Timeline

As with those project managers, it's important that everyone recognize the timeline for change here. You can't change talent in a quarter. This is a tricky point for many business leaders. The American and European business models tend to focus intensely on quarterly results. While you may see some early benefits to workforce planning and talent management, you want everyone to know—from investors down to line managers—that these strategies take time.

If you want to change people's skill set, automate, bring in more contractors, improve your budget, or develop more efficient organization, that takes time. Gathering the data for demand and for supply takes time. Getting that data to speak the same language takes time. Adjusting your models takes time. You can know everything you need to do to act on a particular strategy, but you can't press a button and make that happen overnight. All of those will require time and effort up front.

In particular, time will be spent building up your demand data and developing your forecasts. This is only time-consuming the first time, but there's no way around it when you're just starting out here. Whether it's a matter of weeks or months—depending upon the complexity—your managers will have to do exactly what they did at Apple, fulfilling all their normal responsibilities and spending extra time on this new priority.

When workforce planning goes from red to black depends on the workforce you're working on and your business cycles. I mentioned pharmaceuticals in the last chapter, which can take up to five years before they see the huge gains that are coming. For most companies, you'll clear that line inside of the first three quarters.

You can often break the timeline down like this. The first quarter is dedicated to collecting data, the second quarter to training the data, and the third quarter to seeing some projections.

To see the full benefits of these ideas at the enterprise level, you can expect it to take around two years.

So long as you've secured buy-in from everyone on this, that timeline should be fine. The only issue is disappointed expectations if someone in the organization is expecting faster results.

Scale

After proving the concept with one group, many companies pause and take their workforce planning model companywide. However, as the benefits are seen, wiser leaders notice the potential, scaling and expanding where the pain is greatest.

To find that pain, they often compare themselves to their competitors. For example, Amazon and Microsoft are able to run their server farms with fewer people than Apple. So, if you're Apple, perhaps you wonder why. To truly compete, the old adage still holds, do it better and do it cheaper, and in this example that means beating the giant that is Amazon Web Services.

This is where these models and strategies can really pay off. But to see those benefits you have to scale smart. You have to be consistent in implementation. Don't skip steps. Don't go cheap. It's easier, faster, and cheaper to scale, but it won't be instantaneous. Like Apple, be strategic in where you invest next.

Is there a department that you suspect could deliver faster? Is there somewhere you suspect you could see major savings in labor? Maybe there's a division you know could use more automation. Like Apple, use industry benchmarks to find where these ideas will net the most value. And then the place it will offer the next most value. And expand from there.

Far too often, businesses build processes as they go and develop in an ad hoc manner that suits the moment. Don't let that happen with your workforce planning or talent management.

Because you're going to learn to use muscles you've never used before, this can start out as a challenge. But because this is a standardized process, you can master it. And once you master it, the benefits will continue to show the more you scale.

CHAPTER 10

Making Adjustments

I was part of the team that worked with a major telecommunications company in the UK facing some daunting but not unusual business challenges. Their aim was to offer services across the UK, but they were facing serious competition from larger corporations and from some plucky upstarts. There were changes in technology they had to keep up with, new regulations going into place, and as if that wasn't enough, a new regulator for the industry.

Considering all those challenges, it was no wonder they looked to their workforce to make sure they had the strategy and organization to continue to succeed.

To answer their questions, we followed the entire process covered in this book. We looked at the demand for skills and forecasted forward based on their strategy. We calculated their current supply and found the gaps across the organization—locating around forty opportunities in total. We then considered the best way to fill those gaps, landing on a mix of automation, offshoring, and redeploying skills already located within the company.

It was a great plan, but it wasn't perfect. To get to those predictive powers required not just a single technology to install but regular updates and tweaks to data, as well as adjustments to strategy and talent management processes when the company fell short of the goals set by the workforce planning model.

That wasn't a flaw in the workforce planning process. It was a part of it—a continuous improvement loop if you will. The telecommunications company made astounding progress thanks to the models at their disposal. But that was in part because they knew modeling is not a single solution. It is a tool that requires regular review and improvement.

General Install, Tailored Implementation

To get the kind of results I've referenced throughout this book, you have to do more than just get your company on board and install a system right out of the box. Those are important parts of the process, but there is more that still has to be done. To begin with, you have to add the extra ingredients that customize these models to your company. You have to take active consideration of what your "secret sauce" is: what differentiates you from your competitors.

Consider the differences between Colgate-Palmolive and Procter & Gamble. Both companies make many very similar products. If you go to buy toothpaste, you probably don't care much about the organizational difference between them. But internally, they approach the creation and production of those products in almost opposite ways.

Take a closer look at the boxes of toothpaste next time you're in that aisle, and you'll notice an interesting fact. Almost everything that Colgate-Palmolive makes has the name Colgate or Palmolive on them. But there are few Procter & Gamble products. There is Tide; there is

Swiffer; there is Gillette. To find out who makes those products, you have to look for the little P&G symbol on the packaging somewhere.

The two companies simply have very different philosophies. Both can benefit from a workforce planning system that is largely the same, but they will each have to adapt it to their unique business cultures.

You can roughly break down implementation of this process as 80 percent commonality and 20 percent customization to the specific business philosophies of your organization. The vast majority of what this workforce planning requires is the same across every business and every industry, but don't underestimate the value of that 20 percent.

Culture is what really makes a company distinct. It's central to the difference between Coca-Cola and Pepsi. These differences come up not just in corporate culture but the culture of countries and regions. There are different work cultures in America, India, and China. Those work cultures are different from those in Vietnam and France. And these differences will need to be present in your workforce models.

Most Asian business models look more long term. American business models are often focused on achieving big results as quickly as possible. Workdays can also look different in different cultures. When I worked in China with a large manufacturer, nap time was built into the workday. From twelve to two, the factory was almost completely silent. Everyone rested up because they were expected to work much longer hours.

Different cultures have different expectations for how long an employee stays at a company, how much time they dedicate to their job, and what benefits they should expect. You need to train your models to understand how you intend to do what you do. Otherwise, it can't predict workforce needs for your particular situation.

To see how this works, consider one of the key aspects of workforce planning: location strategy. For decades, companies that do software development have been following a model that is called "chasing the sun." This allows them to create a twenty-four-hour development cycle by chopping up work on key projects and allotting it to different parts of the world. Ideally, they look at the strengths and skills they would find in Silicon Valley (where labor costs are high), India (where they are low), Europe, etc., and divide responsibilities accordingly for shifts that build on one another.

A company might choose to do the "writing" of its software code during the workday in California. When the workday starts in Asia, the lines of code compiled that day then go through testing before being handed off to a development center in eastern Europe that can debug and finalize the code. This would then set up the California team to work on the next section of code when the next workday begins.

To build such teams, workforce planning models have to account for hiring talent in all of these locations and then lay on top of this strategy the regulatory and culture rules that might influence where the company hires. For instance, there is no doubting German engineering prowess. The country's culture and education system produces some of the best engineers on the planet. So if you are going to design things for, say, heavy manufacturing, you would be hard-pressed to find a more capable workforce with which to do the engineering. However, when considering your workforce planning, you would also want to consider that Germany is a high-labor-cost market, that the regulatory environment is such that workers cannot easily (nor cheaply) be let go (so if you are doing something high risk that could cause workforce instability if not successful it may not be the best place to hire workers), and finally, that the German work week is thirty-two hours not the forty of the United States or fifty of China.

Cost, skills, and culture all play a role in hiring considerations here. Weights and measures can be applied to all of these considerations, and they become part of the constraints that are put into the algorithms that underlie the workforce planning calculations in the optimization engine that drives the recommended outcomes.

Of course, once again, none of this automation or optimization from the machine replaces the human element. The machine will spit out a "plan." But at that point, *people* need to actually look at the plan and do a "sanity check" against how the company works or considerations from management that might not easily be translated into code. These workforce planners will then make adjustments and tweaks to the plan before going back to leadership with the plan and selling them on it.

Training the Model and Aligning to Corporate Strategy

Along with training your model on your company's culture, you have to decide the direction you want to take your company. The UK telecom company I worked with knew exactly where they wanted to go. They wanted to beat their biggest competitors, provide better service across the country, and offer the best price for the best-quality product. In other words, they wanted to be the leaders of their industry.

That's the ambition of many of the top companies out there. Audi, for instance, has a clear "lead don't follow" philosophy. They aim to anticipate the trends and to stay ahead of the competition. They want everyone eating their dust, trying to copy what they've already perfected.

But that isn't the only way to run a business. Microsoft isn't necessarily considered a leader in innovation. It doesn't "invent" most of its products; it comes in afterward and develops solutions that integrate with its other products. Microsoft didn't invent word processing, but MS Word is by far the best on the market. Their innovation came on top of something that already existed. The same example could be drawn for spreadsheets, graphical-user-interface-based operating systems, or gaming systems. Often, Microsoft acquires or partners with those leading innovators. And that's been a very successful strategy for them for decades. They didn't invent word processing, spreadsheets, visual operating models, or operating systems. They just made them better and bundled them together.

Likewise, several Japanese and Korean car companies have become huge successes following the lead of companies like Audi. They don't create the trends or innovate much. They focus on manufacturing more cheaply at higher quality and efficiency than those who are leading.

You can follow either of those paths or cut one in between. The value of a workforce plan is that it can tell you what the company is capable of doing today—what the workforce is able to achieve based on current staffing levels and skills. When compared to corporate strategy, you are then able to determine what would be necessary to change the workforce to meet that strategy, and this data can be used to determine if that is indeed the strategy the company wants to follow or if it might want to change it to meet current workforce capabilities. There is no single answer here; it is just providing input so that strategy can be developed in a data-driven manner.

To utilize this tool, though, you have to know which path you intend to take when training your model. To be clear, you absolutely can use your forecast to game out different strategies for your company, but you want to continue to train your model on your company's overall growth philosophy.

Your company is going to invest millions of dollars in their future workforce. Your workforce planning models can help predict where you should spend that money to achieve the results you need, but you have to have a sense of what you want those results to look like.

Review Your Progress

With your direction clear and your models adjusted to your company's culture, you should have your new systems up and running. But you can't just ignore them at that point. You have to continually review your progress, update your data, and adjust your talent management strategies.

Essentially, this involves two processes: grading your company's work and updating your models.

In each step of the talent life cycle, check if your talent management efforts are achieving what the model recommended. What did the model forecast for hiring in each position? What did you actually achieve? If you needed twenty-five people and only hired twenty, why did you fall short?

What did you do to make up for that remaining gap? Did you have to bring in more contractors to supplement? Did you move people over from other departments? Are you happy with those outcomes?

Of those twenty, how many were good hires? Have they stuck around? Are they effective in the jobs they were hired for? Did they have all the skills you assumed they would?

Each of these questions has a grade attached to it to show how well your company is performing in relation to your models.

In training, don't just grade whether everyone attended your trainings; review whether they learned the new skills they need and if they are using those skills. Have the productivity numbers for those who did the training improved? Are they using the new tools you trained them on? Did you have to retrain them?

Do this across every stage of the employee life cycle. Check your promoting capabilities. How many leaders have you advanced? How long has it taken to train and promote a new leader? How quickly do you spot them?

As with all the metrics for demand and supply, you need these grades to be consistent, and you need them in a language that you can feed back into your models.

Ultimately, you are grading yourself on whether you are getting the results you wanted, and you are updating your models so they continue to reflect the reality of your business. Those updates will improve the accuracy of your forecasts for the years ahead.

How often you do these reviews and update your model will depend on your industry. Most industries do this quarterly. Some—like retail and hospitality—do these reviews monthly.

As you do these reviews and update your models, you'll find the model is more accurate and more accurately reflects those elements we've already covered: culture and strategy.

Keep an Eye on Benchmarks

Over the longer term, you'll want to do more than just continually review your own processes and the accuracy of your models' predictions. You'll also want to review the organizational systems within your company. Consider your job titles. Even very disciplined organizations with excellent workforce planning models end up seeing their job families and job titles expand over time. Technology changes, and you add new positions without fully removing the old ones. You enter new markets and create new job titles to match those new needs.

You hire a few all-star people who require new titles to match all their unique responsibilities.

This is inevitable. But from time to time, you want to check those benchmarks again to see how many positions your company has compared to your competitors. There isn't a right or wrong number here, but if you have far more or far fewer, you want to ask questions about why that is.

The same is true for how much you're paying your talent, the average number of days it takes to hire for various positions, and so on. Any time you find numbers outside the averages for your industry, you should investigate whether that is by design and whether it's adding value to your company. If you don't like the answer, you should work to adjust those numbers back to within the standards.

As you do so, continuing to update your models will allow them to pivot and realign to your amended organization. And that will allow their prophetic abilities to continue to offer accurate information as they look into the future.

Trust the Model

Workforce planning is a tool. And it will never be a perfect one. The aim in this game is to reach between 70 and 80 percent accuracy. As I've said throughout this book, you'll never get results that are completely right, and your company will never hit every mark.

But with a little time and investment, you can start using this tool to make improvements across your organization. Within three to six months, your model should see about 50 percent accuracy in the department you've set up in first. Remember, that's 50 percent better than you were six months before. Within three quarters, you should see 70 percent in predictions.

To get beyond 70 percent, though, is a bit harder. It requires you to scale this to the enterprise level. However, keep in mind that every time you expand into a new department, you'll keep seeing that 50 percent improvement within six months. That's excellent ROI.

If you are focused on the goal, you can have the entire model up and running across your company within two years. At that point, you just have to focus on the maintenance we've covered in this chapter.

And then, all that remains is deciding when to pull the trigger on big strategic initiatives. Companies like Moderna were able to develop a COVID vaccine so quickly because they had the playbook in place. They knew how to do it. It was a matter of pulling the trigger. Once the wheels were in motion, the process ran smoothly. The vaccine actually existed within mere months of the virus being identified and genetically mapped. With safety testing and clinical trials, we had a vaccine within the first year for a brand-new disease on the planet.

Of course, that requires trust. But workforce planning has proven time and again that it deserves it. The companies that excelled at doing workforce planning in 2007 and 2008 suffered just like everyone else when the Great Recession hit. Markets were shrinking all over the globe. But they were the first to pivot and adjust to new realities. They moved quickly to work more in economies like Brazil and Russia that were still growing steadily. They put more resources into China.

They had the tools to know where to go, and because they trusted their models, they did better than the companies that went into mass panic, as well as those that just followed trends and those that tried to navigate the crisis by gut instinct alone.

If you build these models and trust them, they can help guide you to the best possible outcomes for your company. Whatever the macroeconomics of the moment, whatever strategy you intend to implement, whatever your industry or company culture—that's the simple truth.

Build it, update it, maintain it, and it can prophesy whatever your talent needs are.

CONCLUSION

There's no one right way to approach talent management and workforce management. You don't have to do it the same way Apple does or Procter & Gamble does. You don't need to emulate Microsoft or a massive telecom company. There are a million variations of these processes, each one unique to the company that employs it.

There is also no single right way to implement these models. Some companies start immediately at enterprise level. Others focus on installing these ideas in one department or initially only build out demand or supply to create clarity around certain needs.

But there is a wrong way to do this, and that's to continue to handle talent by default and to continue to simply do things the same way you always have.

The next step you take is up to you, but if you take nothing else from this book, I hope you'll at least absorb one key idea. It's time to start looking at talent the same way you look at everything else in your organization: as a business metric. Talent is a data-driven process and a driver of business results, just like every other aspect of your company.

From that follows the most powerful and least intuitive idea in this book. To harness the potential of that data, you have to start breaking work down into units of labor. Every other idea in this book is impactful, but nothing revolutionizes a company like that shift in thinking. In fact, I'd say everything else in this book flows out of that concept: talent is a data-driven process, and that data should be measured in units of labor.

Start thinking about the people aspect of your business in this more analytical, more deliberate way, and the rest of the ideas come naturally. You know the supply of resources your company needs and the demand; why not the same for labor? It all comes from that single idea.

That's not to say there's no room for gut instinct in business anymore. It still has a place here, but if you accept the data-driven nature of your talent processes, you can improve results by bolstering your instincts with that data. The more guesswork and intuition you can remove, the more focused your gut can be on the key decisions it still has to make. After all, someone still has to select strategic targets and pull the trigger on major projects. Many people have to act on the information workforce planning models offer up in order to manage talent.

But every part of the process is improved with clearer data on your talent supply, talent demands, and the gap between the two.

Investing in workforce planning and talent management is always money well spent because it takes what differentiates you in the marketplace and strengthens those aspects of your company. If you're a business known for its innovation, you can bring the best innovators in, get them into their ideal place in the company, and keep them there more effectively. If you are known for efficiency, these ideas can improve your efficiency in hiring and training.

That can only improve your identity, your brand, and your outcomes.

In a world flush with new technologies, disrupted markets, and changing worker dynamics, these are tools you can't afford to live without any longer. If you believe in your business, your products, your potential, and your workforce, this is the best ally you could bring into your operations.